Overcoming Delinquent Property Taxes

A Complete Guide to Resolving Tax Debt and Protecting Your Property

Maurice C. Hill

Dedication

To my dear readers who seek knowledge and hope to gain useful information, including those who face financial difficulties and struggle to pay their property taxes. This book is dedicated to all of you.

Despite the challenges you face, your hunger for learning and growth is a testament to the resilient spirit of the human mind. Whether you are seeking practical advice, exploring new ideas, or simply looking to broaden your horizons, I hope this book will provide you with the insights and tools you need to succeed, even in the face of financial adversity. I understand the burden you carry, and I am here to offer support.

I am grateful for your unwavering determination, open-mindedness, and willingness to engage with the world around you, despite the financial obstacles you encounter. Your quest for understanding, despite the financial constraints, inspires me, and I am honored to be a small part of your journey. May this book serve as a guide and a companion as you navigate the challenges and opportunities of life, including the struggles with property taxes.

May it provide you with the information, inspiration, and support you need to achieve your goals and fulfill your dreams while also addressing the financial difficulties you may face. Thank you for choosing to spend your time with me and sharing my passion for learning and discovery, regardless of your financial circumstances.

With warmth and gratitude,

Maurice C. Hill

Acknowledgment

I would like to take a moment to express my deepest gratitude to Attorney Monique Reynolds for her unwavering support and belief in me throughout the creation of this book, "Overcoming Delinquent Property Taxes: A Complete Guide to Resolving Tax Debt and Protecting Your Property." Her encouragement, feedback, and legal expertise have played an integral role in shaping the content of this book. With her invaluable contributions, the complexities of overcoming delinquent property taxes have gained clarity and depth.

I also extend my heartfelt appreciation to my exceptional editor, whose keen eye, meticulous attention to detail, and unwavering support have transformed this manuscript into something truly remarkable. Their guidance and expertise have ensured the effectiveness and clarity of the concepts presented within these pages.

In addition, I would like to acknowledge the incredible team at One United Publishing, whose dedication and support have been integral to the realization of this book. Their professionalism and unwavering commitment to excellence have paved the way for this work to reach your hands.

Now, dear reader, it is with great excitement and anticipation that I invite you to embark on this journey with me. Together, let us navigate the intricate world of delinquent property taxes and forge a path toward financial stability and the protection of your property. May this book serve as a beacon of hope, knowledge, and empowerment as you overcome the challenges that lie within delinquent property taxes or as you assist others in doing so.

With heartfelt gratitude,

Maurice C. Hill

Contents

Prologue

Dear Reader,

Welcome to the world of possibilities and empowerment that awaits you within the pages of "Overcoming Delinquent Property Taxes: A Complete Guide to Resolving Tax Debt and Protecting Your Property." As you embark on this transformative journey, allow me, Maurice C. Hill, to introduce myself and share the driving forces behind the creation of this book.

With decades of experience as a licensed real estate broker, I have had the privilege of assisting individuals in navigating various real estate challenges. Throughout my career, I have witnessed firsthand the profound impact that property tax issues can have on the lives and aspirations of property owners.

Motivated by an unwavering commitment to empower individuals with invaluable real estate knowledge, the seed of this comprehensive guide took root within me as an unshakable conviction. I have seen the stark contrast between homeowners who faced overwhelming financial challenges and those who thrived, a distinction often attributed to the presence or absence of information. It is with great purpose and determination that I present this book, offering essential information specifically tailored to address property tax issues.

Within the following pages, you will discover a wealth of knowledge and insights that I have gathered throughout my extensive real estate career. The purpose of this book is to equip you with the necessary tools, strategies, and understanding to navigate the treacherous waters of delinquent property taxes. My sincerest desire is to empower you to uphold the dream of homeownership, even in the face of tax-related obstacles.

Throughout this comprehensive guide, you can expect an in-depth exploration of the topic at hand. We will delve into understanding the intricacies of property tax assessments and rates, unravel the appeal process, and shed light on available tax exemptions. You will gain insights into the consequences of unpaid property taxes, comprehend the implications of liens on your property, and discover effective strategies for resolving tax debt while safeguarding one of your most valuable assets.

It is my hope that this book will serve as your trusted companion, offering clarity and guidance as you navigate the complex realm of delinquent property taxes. By arming yourself with knowledge, you will gain the confidence to take action and overcome the challenges that may lie ahead. Remember, the power to protect your property and secure your financial well-being is within your grasp.

I invite you to embark on this journey of discovery and

empowerment, knowing that you are not alone. Together, let us navigate the intricate path toward resolving tax debt and protecting what matters most to you—your property. May this book be a beacon of knowledge, empowerment, and hope as you embark on this transformative endeavor.

With warm regards,

Maurice C. Hill

Chapter One

Property Tax and Homeownership

Property taxes are a necessary part of homeownership, collected annually by local government entities, and are based on the value of the property. These taxes fund essential local services such as schools, police and fire departments, and infrastructure improvements. In this chapter, we will delve into the details of property taxes, including their collection, use, and calculation.

Homeowners are responsible for paying property taxes, and failing to do so can result in late fees, interest charges, and even property foreclosure. The money collected through property taxes is used to fund a wide range of local services and initiatives, including public schools, roads, parks and recreation facilities, and emergency services. It is an important source of revenue for local governments, ensuring that communities have the resources they need to provide essential services and support to residents.

In the next section of this chapter, we will explore the differences between property taxes and rent taxes and their impact on property owners and renters. Understanding these differences is crucial for making informed financial decisions. By staying on top of property tax payments and understanding their importance, homeowners can contribute to improving their community and protecting their financial well-being.

Property taxes are a type of tax imposed by local government entities on real estate properties within their jurisdiction. The amount of property tax owed is typically based on the value of the property and can be used to fund a variety of local services such as schools, police and fire departments, and infrastructure improvements.

Property taxes are typically collected by the local government on an annual basis, either through the mail or in person at a local tax collector's office. The property owner is responsible for paying the tax bill, and failure to do so can result in late fees, interest charges, and even the potential for property foreclosure.

The money collected through property taxes is used to fund a wide range of local services and initiatives. This can include funding for public schools, roads and highways, parks and recreation facilities, and emergency services such as police and fire departments. Property taxes can also be used to fund public services like libraries, community centers, and public health initiatives.

In some cases, property taxes may also be used to fund special initiatives or projects, such as the restoration of historical buildings or the construction of new public facilities. It is important to note that property taxes are an important source of revenue for local governments and play a critical role in ensuring that communities have the resources they need to provide essential services and support to residents.

Property taxes and rent taxes are two distinct forms of taxation that are often confused. In contrast to property taxes, rent tax is a tax on the rental income a property owner earns. This tax is usually levied by the state or federal government and is calculated as a percentage of the rent collected. Rent taxes are usually paid by the property owner and are used to fund a wider range of government services, such as social security and national defense. Unlike property taxes, rent taxes are not tied to the value of the property and can fluctuate with changes in the rental market.

Overall, property taxes and rent taxes serve different purposes and are levied at different levels of government. Property taxes fund local government services, while rent taxes provide revenue for larger, more comprehensive government programs. Both types of taxes play an important role in financing government services and can impact both property owners and renters in different ways.

The calculation of property taxes is typically performed by tax assessors, who the local government appoints. Tax assessors use a variety of methods to determine the value of a property for tax purposes, including consideration of factors such as the size and location of the property, the quality of its construction, and any improvements that have been made. One common method used by tax assessors is a market analysis, where they compare the property in question to similar properties that have recently been sold in the area. They then use this information to estimate the market value of the property, which is used as the basis for calculating the property tax owed.

In addition to market analysis, tax assessors may also use other methods to determine the value of a property, such as a cost approach, which estimates the cost of replacing the property with a similar one, or the income approach, which calculates the property's value based on its potential rental income.

Once the value of the property has been determined, the tax assessor will multiply the value by the local property tax rate to arrive at the amount of property tax owed. Property tax rates can vary widely between jurisdictions, and they are often adjusted annually to ensure that the local government has sufficient revenue to provide public services.

For example, let's say that a property has been assessed to have a market value of $300,000. The local property tax rate is 1.5%. To calculate the property tax owed, the tax assessor would multiply the market value ($300,000) by the property tax rate (1.5%): $300,000 * 0.015 = $4,500. This means the property owner would owe $4,500 in property taxes each year. If the local government were to increase the property tax rate to 2%, the property owner's tax bill would increase to $6,000 ($300,000 * 0.02 = $6,000). Conversely, if the local government were to decrease the property tax rate to 1%, the property owner's tax bill would decrease to $3,000 ($300,000 * 0.01 = $3,000).

As a homeowner, it's important to be knowledgeable about property taxes, as they can have a significant impact on your financial situation. Homeowners should familiarize themselves with the following aspects of property taxes:

- Assessment value: The assessed value of your property is used to calculate your property tax bill. Make sure that the assessed value is accurate and reflects any improvements or changes that have been made to your property.

- Tax rate: Property tax rates can vary widely between jurisdictions. Familiarize yourself with the local property tax rate and how it is determined, as it will impact the amount of property taxes you owe.

- Appeal process: If you believe that the assessed value of your property is incorrect, you have the right to appeal the assessment. Learn about the appeals process in your jurisdiction and the steps you need to take to initiate an appeal.

- Tax exemptions: Some homeowners may be eligible for property tax exemptions, such as those for veterans, seniors, or those with low incomes. Familiarize yourself with the exemptions available in your jurisdiction and whether you are eligible for any of them.

- Payment options: Property taxes are typically due annually, and you may have the option to pay them in full or in installments. Learn about the payment options available in your jurisdiction and the deadlines for payment.

By being familiar with these aspects of property taxes, homeowners can better understand their tax bill and take steps to manage their property tax obligation.

Tax assessors have a critical role in the property tax system. They are responsible for determining the assessed value of properties, which is used to calculate property tax bills. To ensure accuracy, tax assessors must consider factors such as the size and location of the property, the quality of its construction, and any improvements that have been made. They must also be familiar with local property tax rates and any exemptions that may be available to homeowners.

In addition, tax assessors must be familiar with the appeal process and be able to provide clear and accurate information to homeowners who may wish to challenge the assessed value of their property. By performing their duties accurately and transparently, tax assessors can help to ensure that the property tax system is fair and equitable for all homeowners.

In conclusion, property taxes are a necessary and important part of homeownership. They are a type of tax imposed by local government entities on real estate properties within their jurisdiction, and they are used to fund a wide range of local services and initiatives. By paying property taxes, homeowners contribute to their community and ensure that essential services and infrastructure are maintained.

Homeowners need to know how property taxes are calculated and what factors affect their property tax bills. They should familiarize themselves with the assessment value of their property, the local property tax rate, the appeals process, tax exemptions, and payment options. By being knowledgeable about these aspects of property taxes, homeowners can better understand their tax bills and take steps to manage their property tax obligation.

Finally, it is important to note that property taxes and rent taxes are two distinct forms of taxation that impact property owners and renters differently. While property taxes fund local government services, rent taxes provide revenue for larger, more comprehensive government programs. By understanding the differences between these two forms of taxation, homeowners and renters can better navigate the complex world of taxation and make informed decisions about their financial future.

Chapter Two

The Impact of a Lien on Your Property: What You Need to Know

Property liens are an important aspect of property ownership, and property owners need to be aware of the various types of liens that can be placed on their property. This chapter will discuss the different types of property liens, including voluntary and non-consensual liens, and specific types of liens such as attachment, judgment, child support, property tax, IRS, family law real property, homeowner's association, possessory, and UCC liens. We will also explore how liens can impact a property owner's financial situation and how creditors collect on them. It's crucial for property owners to understand the implications of liens on their assets and credit score and to take immediate action if a lien is filed against their property. By understanding how liens work, property owners can take steps to protect their assets and financial well-being. In the next section of this chapter, we will delve into how creditors collect on liens and what steps property owners can take to address the situation if a lien is filed against their property.

A property lien is a legal claim made by a creditor on a property owned by a debtor as security for a debt. Property liens have a long history and have been used in various forms for centuries as a means of ensuring that debts are paid.

Overcoming Delinquent Property Taxes

In the past, property liens were often used by governments as a way of collecting taxes owed by property owners. If a property owner failed to pay their taxes, the government would place a lien on the property, effectively preventing the owner from selling or using the property until the debt was paid. This provided a strong incentive for property owners to pay their taxes, as they would otherwise risk losing their property.

In modern times, property liens are often used by banks and other creditors to secure loans. For example, when a homeowner takes out a mortgage to purchase a property, the bank will typically place a lien on the property as security for the loan. If the homeowner fails to repay the loan, the bank can foreclose on the property, effectively taking ownership and selling it to recoup its losses.

In addition to being used to secure loans, property liens can also be used in a variety of other contexts, such as to secure payment for work performed on a property, to collect fines for building code violations, or to secure payment of outstanding debts such as utility bills.

It's important to be aware of the potential impact of property liens on a property owner's financial situation. Property liens can make it difficult to sell a property, as potential buyers may be reluctant to purchase a property that is encumbered by a lien.

Additionally, property liens can significantly reduce the value of a property, as they can make it difficult to obtain financing or insurance.

Ultimately, property liens have a long history and have been used as a means of securing debts and ensuring that they are paid. Owners of various forms of real estate should be aware of the potential impact of property liens on their financial situation and take steps to ensure that they are in good standing with creditors and avoid having liens placed on their properties.

Understanding Voluntary Liens: What You Need to Know

Voluntary liens are voluntarily placed on a property by the property owner as security for a loan or other debt. Unlike involuntary liens, which are placed on a property without the owner's consent, voluntary liens are entered into voluntarily by the property owner as a way to secure financing or other debts.

Examples of voluntary liens include:

1. Mortgages: A mortgage is a common type of voluntary lien that is used to secure a loan for the purchase of a property. The property owner voluntarily places a lien on the property as security for the loan, allowing the lender to foreclose on the property if the loan is not repaid as agreed.

2. Home Equity Loans: A home equity loan is a type of loan that allows homeowners to use the equity in their property as

collateral. By placing a voluntary lien on the property, the homeowner secures the loan and agrees to repay the loan with interest.

3. Personal Loans: In some cases, property owners may use their property as collateral to secure a personal loan. The property owner voluntarily places a lien on the property as security for the loan, allowing the lender to foreclose on the property if the loan is not repaid as agreed.

4. Contractor Liens: In some cases, property owners may use their property as collateral to secure payment for work performed by contractors. The contractor may place a voluntary lien on the property as security for payment, allowing them to foreclose on the property if the owner fails to pay for the work as agreed.

Voluntary liens can provide property owners with access to financing or other funds that they may not otherwise be able to obtain. However, it's important to be aware of the potential consequences of voluntarily placing a lien on a property, including the possibility of losing the property if the loan is not repaid as agreed. Before entering into a loan agreement that involves a voluntary lien, property owners should carefully consider the terms of the loan and the risks involved.

A voluntary lien is created when a debtor takes action, such as obtaining a mortgage loan to purchase real estate. This type of lien is consensual and is established through a contractual agreement between the debtor and the creditor. Other common examples of voluntary liens include car loans, where the lien is recorded on the vehicle title. These types of liens serve as security for the debt and provide the creditor with a legal claim to the property in the event that the debt is not repaid as agreed.

- **Non-Consensual Liens**, also known as involuntary liens, are liens that are placed on a property without the owner's consent. These types of liens are typically imposed by a government entity, such as the Internal Revenue Service (IRS) or a local tax authority, to secure payment of taxes, fines, or other debts the property owner owes. Unlike voluntary liens, which are entered voluntarily by the property owner to secure financing or other debts, non-consensual liens are imposed against the owner's will. The property owner is typically notified of the lien and given an opportunity to dispute or pay the debt, but failure to do so can result in the sale of the property to satisfy the debt.

- **An Attachment Lien** is placed on the property to secure payment of a debt. This type of lien is often used in cases where the creditor has not been able to collect payment from the debtor through other means, such as wage garnishment or bank account levies. The attachment lien gives the creditor the right to seize and sell the property to satisfy the debt. In some cases, the attachment lien may be imposed without the owner's consent, while in others, the owner may voluntarily agree to the lien as a way to secure payment of the debt.

- **A Judgment Lien** is a legal claim against a property that is imposed as a result of a court judgment. This type of lien is typically imposed when a creditor obtains a court order requiring the debtor to pay a debt, and the debtor fails to do so. The judgment lien gives the creditor the right to seize and sell the property to satisfy the debt. In some cases, the judgment lien may be imposed without the owner's consent, while in others, the owner may voluntarily agree to the lien as a way to secure payment of the debt.

- **A Child Support Lien** is imposed to secure payment of past-due child support. This type of lien is typically imposed by a government agency, such as the Department of Child Support Services, when the obligor (the parent responsible for paying child support) falls behind on payments. The child support lien gives the agency the right to seize and sell the property to satisfy the debt. In some cases, the child support lien may be imposed without the owner's consent, while in others, the owner may voluntarily agree to the lien as a way to secure payment of the debt.

- **A Property Tax Lien** is a legal claim against a property imposed to secure payment of property taxes owed to a government entity, such as a city or county. This type of lien is typically imposed when the property owner fails to pay property taxes in a timely manner. The property tax lien gives the government entity the right to seize and sell the property to satisfy the debt. In some cases, the property tax lien may be imposed without the owner's consent, while in others, the owner may voluntarily agree to the lien as a way to secure payment of the debt.

- **An Internal Revenue Service (IRS)** lien is a legal claim against a property imposed to secure payment of federal taxes owed to the United States government. This type of lien is typically imposed when an individual or business fails to pay federal taxes in a timely manner. The IRS lien gives the government the right to seize and sell the property to satisfy the debt. In some cases, the IRS lien may be imposed without the owner's consent, while in others, the owner may voluntarily agree to the lien as a way to secure payment of the debt.

- **A Mechanics Lien** is a legal claim against a property imposed to secure payment for services or materials provided to improve the property. This type of lien is typically imposed by contractors, subcontractors, suppliers, or other service providers who have not been paid for their work or materials. The mechanics lien gives the claimant the right to seize and sell the property to satisfy the debt. In some cases, the mechanics lien may be imposed without the owner's consent, while in others, the owner may voluntarily agree to the lien as a way to secure payment of the debt.

- A **Family Law Real Property Lien** is a legal claim against a property that is imposed to secure payment of debts related to family law matters, such as divorce settlements, spousal support, or child support. This type of lien is typically imposed by court order and gives the party entitled to pay the right to seize and sell the property to satisfy the debt. In some cases, the family law real property lien may be imposed without the owner's consent, while in others, the owner may voluntarily agree to the lien as a way to secure payment of the debt.

- **A Homeowners Association (HOA) Lien** is a legal claim against a property that is imposed to secure payment of outstanding dues or assessments owed to the HOA. The HOA typically imposes this type of lien to enforce its governing documents, which typically require owners to pay HOA dues and assessments in a timely manner. The HOA lien gives the HOA the right to seize and sell the property to satisfy the debt. In some cases, the HOA lien may be imposed without the owner's consent, while in others, the owner may voluntarily agree to the lien as a way to secure payment of the debt.

- A **Possessory Lien** is a legal claim against a property that is imposed to secure payment for services or materials provided for the property. This type of lien is typically imposed by those who have possession of the property, such as a mechanic who has repaired a car or a storage facility that has stored personal property. The possessory lien gives the claimant the right to seize and sell the property to satisfy the debt. In some cases, the possessory lien may be imposed without the owner's consent, while in others, the owner may voluntarily agree to the lien as a way to secure payment of the debt.

- A **UCC Lien**, also known as a Uniform Commercial Code lien, is a legal claim against personal property that is imposed to secure payment for goods or services provided in the course of a commercial transaction. This type of lien is recognized under the Uniform Commercial Code, a set of laws that governs commercial transactions in the United States. The UCC lien gives the claimant the right to seize and sell personal property to satisfy the debt. In some cases, the UCC lien may be imposed without the owner's consent, while in others, the owner may voluntarily agree to the lien as a way to secure payment of the debt.

All these liens affect can have a significant impact on the owner's ability to sell or use the property and can negatively impact the owner's credit score. Remember that it is very important for property owners to understand their rights and obligations with respect to UCC liens and to take appropriate steps to address any debts that may result in the imposition of a lien.

The Impact of Liens on Your Property: What You Need to Know

When a lien is placed on a property, it typically restricts the owner's ability to sell or transfer ownership of the property. This can make it more difficult for the owner to sell the property or to access the equity in the property. Additionally, a lien may make it difficult for the owner to refinance the property or obtain additional financing.

A lien can also negatively impact the owner's credit score. Liens are public records, and they are often reported to credit bureaus. The presence of a lien on a property can make it more difficult for the owner to obtain new credit or refinance existing debt.

It is important for property owners to be aware of any liens that may be placed on their property. If a lien is imposed, the owner should take steps to address the underlying debt and resolve the lien. This may involve negotiating a payment plan with the creditor, paying off the debt, or seeking the help of a legal professional.

In some cases, a lien may be imposed without the owner's knowledge. In such cases, it is important for the owner to take prompt action to address the lien and to clear up any misunderstandings that may have led to the imposition of the lien.

Overall, liens can have a significant impact on a property and its owner, and it is important for property owners to understand the impact of liens and to take appropriate steps to address any debts that may result in the imposition of a lien.

Collecting on Liens: Strategies and Methods Used by Creditors

When a creditor places a lien on a property, it is usually to secure payment for a debt that the property owner owes. In some cases, the creditor may seek to collect on the lien in order to recover the debt.

One common way for a creditor to collect on a lien is through the sale of the property. If the property owner fails to pay the debt that is secured by the lien, the creditor may initiate a foreclosure sale of the property. The proceeds of the sale are used to pay off the debt and any other costs associated with the sale. An example of a creditor collecting on a lien through the sale of the property is as follows: John, a homeowner, fell behind on his property tax payments and as a result, the county filed a tax lien against his property. John was unable to pay off the tax debt, and the county initiated a foreclosure sale of his property. The property was sold at auction, and the proceeds from the sale were used to pay off the tax debt and any other associated costs. Unfortunately, the sale of the property did not cover the full amount of the tax debt, and John was left with a remaining balance to pay. This experience was a harsh lesson for John, who realized the importance of staying on top of his property tax payments to avoid the risk of foreclosure.

Another way for a creditor to collect on a lien is by negotiating a payment plan with the property owner. In some cases, the creditor may agree to a payment plan that allows the owner to pay off the debt over time while continuing to live in the property. Let's say John is a property owner in California who fell behind on his property tax payments. The county government placed a tax lien on his property and warned him that his property might face foreclosure if he did not pay the taxes. However, John does not have the funds to pay off the full amount of taxes immediately.

In this situation, John could negotiate a payment plan with the county government. The government may agree to a plan allowing John to pay off the debt over time while continuing to live on the property. For example, John may agree to pay a certain amount each month in addition to his regular property tax payments until the debt is fully paid off.

By agreeing to a payment plan, John can avoid the risk of foreclosure and keep his property. However, it's important to note that the terms of the payment plan will depend on the specific situation and the creditor's willingness to negotiate.

In some cases, a creditor may also seek a court order that allows them to collect on the lien by taking control of the property or by garnishing the property owner's wages. This typically requires a court judgment, and the creditor must follow the legal process for collecting the debt. An example of a creditor seeking a court order to collect on a lien could be a homeowner who falls behind on their mortgage payments and the lender initiates a foreclosure proceeding. The lender would need to follow the legal process, which typically involves filing a lawsuit, obtaining a court judgment, and ultimately seizing the property or garnishing the borrower's wages to collect the outstanding debt. This process can be lengthy and costly for both the lender and the borrower, so it's important for property owners to stay current on their payments and work with their lender to avoid default and potential legal action.

It is important for property owners to understand their rights and responsibilities when it comes to liens and debt collection. If a lien is imposed, the owner should take steps to address the underlying debt and resolve the lien. This may involve negotiating a payment plan with the creditor, paying off the debt, or seeking the help of a legal professional.

Overall, the process for collecting on a lien can be complex, and property owners need to be informed about their rights and to take appropriate steps to address any debts that may result in the imposition of a lien.

Responding to Property Liens: Steps to Take When a Lien is Filed on Your Property

If a lien is filed on your property, it is important to take immediate action to address the issue. A lien can have a major impact on your ability to sell the property or access credit, and it can also affect your credit score.

The first step is to determine the reason for the lien. This may involve reviewing the documents associated with the lien and contacting the party that filed the lien to request additional information.

If the lien is related to a debt, it is important to take steps to resolve the debt as soon as possible. This may involve negotiating a payment plan with the creditor, paying off the debt in full, or seeking the help of a legal professional.

If the lien is incorrect or unjustified, you may need to take legal action to have the lien removed. This may involve disputing the lien with the party that filed it or seeking the help of a legal professional.

Regardless of the reason for the lien, keeping good records and documentation related to the issue is important. This may include copies of correspondence, receipts, and any other relevant documents.

It is also important to keep in mind that the process of resolving a lien can be complex and time-consuming, and it may be necessary to seek the help of a legal professional. This can help ensure that your rights are protected and that the lien is resolved promptly and effectively.

In summary, if a lien is issued against your property, you must move quickly to settle the matter and preserve your rights and interests.

Can Creditors Place a Lien on Your House? Exploring Your Rights and Protections

Yes, a creditor can put a lien on your house in certain circumstances. A lien is a legal claim on a property that serves as security for a debt owed to a creditor. When a lien is placed on your house, it means that the creditor has a right to your property and can take steps to collect the debt, including selling the property.

As a reminder, there are various types of liens that can be placed on a property, and each type serves a specific purpose. For instance, tax liens are imposed by the government to secure payment of outstanding property taxes. An example of this would be a property owner who fails to pay their annual property taxes, and as a result, the government places a lien on the property until the taxes are paid. Another type of lien is a judgment lien, which results from a court order in a lawsuit.

For example, if a person is sued and the court orders them to pay damages to the plaintiff, a lien may be placed on the person's property to secure payment of the judgment. Lastly, mechanic's liens are used by contractors and other service providers to secure payment for work performed on the property. An example of this would be a contractor who performs renovations on a property but is not paid for their work. The contractor can place a lien on the property, which will prevent the property owner from selling or refinancing the property until the debt is paid off.

In order to place a lien on your house, a creditor must follow certain legal procedures, including providing notice to the property owner and filing the lien with the appropriate government authority. The specifics of these procedures vary depending on the type of lien and the laws of the jurisdiction where the property is located.

It is important to note that not all liens on a property are valid or enforceable. In some cases, a lien may be invalid if it was not properly filed or placed on the property without the owner's knowledge. In such cases, it may be possible to have the lien removed. An example of an invalid or unenforceable lien could be if a contractor files a mechanic's lien on a property but fails to properly notify the property owner within the required timeframe. Alternatively, if a lien is filed on a property that the creditor does not have a legal right to claim, such as a lien on a property owned solely by one spouse for a debt owed by the other spouse, the lien may be invalid, and could potentially be removed.

Overall, a creditor can put a lien on your house if you owe a debt, and the creditor has the right to secure payment through a lien. Consider the following, if you have taken out a home equity loan and have fallen behind on your payments, the lender may place a lien on your property to secure the debt. If you continue to miss payments, the lender may eventually initiate foreclosure proceedings, which can result in the loss of your home. However, if you are proactive and work with the lender to come up with a repayment plan or explore other options, such as refinancing, you may be able to resolve the debt and prevent a lien from being placed on your property. It is essential to understand the legal requirements and options available to you when dealing with a potential lien on your property to avoid any negative consequences.

Understanding the legal requirements for placing a lien on a property is crucial to prevent any wrongful or invalid liens. Creditors must follow proper legal procedures and meet specific requirements to place a valid lien on a property. Property owners should also be aware of their rights and protections under the law regarding liens on their property.

In the case of disputes or challenges to a lien, it is essential to seek legal guidance to ensure that your rights are protected and that the dispute is resolved in a timely and fair manner. Delays in resolving liens can result in mounting debts, legal fees, and the risk of foreclosure or other serious consequences. Taking proactive steps to resolve any liens or disputes related to a property lien can help property owners avoid the negative consequences associated with liens and ensure their financial stability.

Determining Property Liens: How to Find Out If There Is a Lien Against a Property You Own

To determine if there is a lien against your property, you can take a few steps. One of the easiest ways is to perform a title search on your property. Let's say you're a property owner who wants to determine if there are any liens on your property. You can start by performing a title search. You could either go to your local county or state records office and request a title search or hire a title search company to do it for you. The title search will provide you with information about any liens or encumbrances on your property, including the type of lien and the creditor who filed it. For example, you might find out that there is a tax lien on your property filed by the IRS, indicating unpaid federal taxes. Knowing this information can help you take appropriate steps to resolve the lien in a timely manner and avoid any potential legal consequences.

Another way to determine if there is a lien against your property is to check with the appropriate government authority. One of the simplest ways is to contact the appropriate government entity. For example, if you believe there may be a tax lien on your property, you can contact the local tax assessor's office to request information about any outstanding property taxes. Similarly, if you suspect that there may be a judgment lien on your property, you can check with the local court records office. These government agencies can provide you with important information about the lien, including the type of lien, the creditor who filed it, and the amount owed. It is important to keep in mind that not all liens are recorded with the government, so it is also a good idea to perform a title search or hire a title search company to ensure that you have a comprehensive understanding of any potential liens on your property.

It is important to regularly check for liens on your property, as new liens can be placed at any time. For example, if you miss a payment on a mortgage loan, the lender may file a lien on your property to secure payment of the debt. If you are in the process of selling your property, a title search will be performed as part of the transaction, and any liens or encumbrances on your property will be revealed.

In conclusion, property liens are a common aspect of property ownership, and it's important for property owners to be aware of the different types of liens that can be placed on their property. Voluntary liens, such as mortgages and home equity loans, are created with the owner's consent, while non-consensual liens are placed on a property without the owner's consent.

Various types of liens, including attachment liens, judgment liens, child support liens, property tax liens, IRS liens, family law real property liens, homeowners association (HOA) liens, possessory liens, and UCC liens, can have different impacts on property owner's financial situation. It's important for property owners to understand the potential consequences of each type of lien and take action to address the situation if a lien is filed against their property.

By understanding the impact of liens on their property and their financial situation, property owners can take steps to protect their assets and their credit score. Being knowledgeable about property liens can also help property owners make informed decisions about their financial future and ensure that their property remains a valuable asset for years to come.

Chapter Three

The Consequences of Unpaid Property Taxes

Paying property taxes is not just a responsibility but also an essential part of owning a property. Unfortunately, not all property owners take this responsibility seriously, and the consequences of failing to pay property taxes can be severe. From penalties and foreclosure to legal and financial consequences, the ramifications of not paying property taxes can be catastrophic.

In this chapter, we will dive into the outcomes of not paying property taxes, including the distribution of funds from foreclosure, avoidance actions, and alternatives to foreclosure. We will explore the reasons behind property tax delinquency and the options available for those who are unable to keep their home. It is crucial for property owners to understand the potential consequences of not paying property taxes on time and take the necessary steps to prevent such outcomes.

But what if property owners are struggling to keep up with their tax payments? What if they are faced with unforeseen circumstances that make it difficult to pay their taxes? Is there a way out of the situation, or are they destined to lose their property?

As we delve deeper into this chapter, we will play devil's advocate and examine both sides of the coin. We will provide readers with the knowledge they need to understand the consequences of unpaid property taxes fully. At the same time, we will explore the potential options available to those who find themselves in a difficult financial situation.

So, if you are a property owner struggling to keep up with your tax payments or are merely curious about the potential consequences of not paying property taxes on time, then this chapter is for you. Let us guide you through the potential outcomes of unpaid property taxes and help you make informed decisions to protect your property and financial well-being.

When property owners fail to pay their property taxes, they open the door to a range of potential consequences from the government. To begin with, the government may place a tax lien on the property, giving them a legal right to the property until the taxes are paid. This can have a negative impact on the owner's ability to sell or refinance the property. Moreover, if the owner does not pay the taxes, the government may choose to seize the property and sell it at a tax sale in order to recover the owed taxes. This could result in the loss of ownership of the property and any equity the owner may have had in it.

To avoid these dire consequences, property owners should ensure they stay current on their property tax payments. If they are unable to pay, they may be able to work out a payment plan with the government or apply for a property tax reduction. It is also important for property owners to regularly review their property tax records for accuracy to prevent any unexpected surprises and to have time to address any issues before they escalate into serious problems. Owners can protect their property and preserve their financial interests by staying informed and current on their property tax obligations.

The Consequences of Late or Unpaid Property Taxes: Understanding Penalties and Fees

When property owners fail to pay their property taxes, they risk facing a number of penalties and consequences, including interest charges and additional fees that can accumulate over time. This can make it more difficult for them to catch up on the payments and can negatively affect their credit score, making it harder to secure loans or credit in the future.

In some cases, the government may place a lien on the property, giving them the right to seize and sell the property to recoup the unpaid taxes. This can have a major impact on the property owner's ability to sell or refinance the property, as the lien must be satisfied before any transaction can be completed. It can also negatively affect the owner's credit score, making it difficult to secure future financing.

If the property owner continues to neglect their tax obligations, the government may initiate foreclosure proceedings, which could result in the loss of the property. This can have long-lasting consequences on the property owner's credit score and their ability to secure housing or credit in the future.

It is important for property owners to take these penalties and consequences seriously and to take action to address the issue as soon as possible. This includes staying current on their property tax payments, working out payment plans with the government if necessary, and regularly checking their property tax records to ensure they are up-to-date and accurate. By doing so, property owners can avoid potential financial hardship and protect their investment in their property.

Foreclosure: Understanding the Process and Implications for Property Owners

When it comes to property ownership, paying taxes is a crucial responsibility that should not be taken lightly. However, unforeseen circumstances may arise, causing you to fall behind on your property tax payments. If this happens, you risk facing a foreclosure, which can have devastating consequences for your financial future.

Foreclosure is the legal process by which the government takes possession of a property due to the homeowner's failure to pay property taxes. This process can be initiated by the government issuing a notice of default, informing the homeowner that they are in default of their property tax payments and urging them to take action to rectify the situation.

If the homeowner fails to pay the taxes or make arrangements to do so, the government may start foreclosure proceedings. This involves the government filing a lawsuit and obtaining a court order to seize the property and sell it in order to recoup the unpaid taxes. The process can be lengthy, taking several months or even years to reach completion, during which time the homeowner may be evicted from the property, and the property may be listed for sale.

The consequences of foreclosure can be severe, including the loss of the property and a negative impact on the homeowner's credit score. That's why it's essential to avoid foreclosure and address any property tax issues as soon as possible. Seeking the advice of a financial advisor, a tax professional, or an attorney can be beneficial. They can help you understand your rights and obligations, provide guidance on the best course of action, and help you protect your financial future.

It's important to understand that foreclosure can have a significant impact on your life, both financially and emotionally. Taking proactive steps to prevent it can make a world of difference. Staying current on property tax payments, regularly checking property tax records, and seeking professional advice when needed are all essential steps in avoiding foreclosure and ensuring a stable financial future.

Distribution of Funds in a Foreclosure Sale: How Proceeds Are Allocated

When a property owner fails to pay their property taxes or other liens, the government may foreclose on the property and sell it to recoup the unpaid debts. The sale of the property generates funds that are typically used to pay off outstanding debts and liens. However, the distribution of these funds can vary depending on the jurisdiction and local laws and regulations.

In most cases, the funds are first used to pay off the outstanding taxes owed on the property. This includes any delinquent property taxes, penalties, and interest that may have accrued over time. Once the taxes are paid off, any remaining funds are typically used to pay off other liens or debts on the property, such as mortgage loans or mechanics liens.

The order in which liens are paid can vary depending on the jurisdiction and the type of lien involved. In some cases, tax liens may have priority over other types of liens and be paid off first. In other cases, other liens, such as mortgage loans, may have priority over tax liens.

After all of the outstanding debts and liens have been paid, any remaining funds are usually returned to the former property owner or their estate if the owner has passed away. However, it is important to note that in some cases, the sale of the foreclosed property may not generate enough funds to pay off all of the outstanding debts and liens. In such cases, the debts and liens may remain outstanding, and the creditor may still have the right to collect on them.

Strategies for Avoiding Foreclosure: Taking Action to Protect Your Property

There are several potential foreclosure e avoidance actions that homeowners can take to prevent the loss of their property. These actions include:

- Loan modification: Negotiating with the lender to change the terms of the loan, such as the interest rate, monthly payment, or loan length, in order to make payments more affordable.

- Refinancing: Obtaining a new loan with more favorable terms to pay off the existing loan, including property taxes.

- Deed in lieu of foreclosure: Voluntarily transferring ownership of the property to the lender in exchange for releasing the mortgage obligation.

- Short sale: Selling the property for less than the amount owed, with the lender agreeing to accept the lesser amount as full payment.

- Bankruptcy: Filing for bankruptcy can provide temporary protection from foreclosure proceedings, allowing the homeowner to reorganize their debts and potentially negotiate with the lender.

It's important for homeowners to take action as soon as possible if they're unable to pay their property taxes or are facing the possibility of foreclosure. Seeking the advice of a financial advisor, real estate attorney, or housing counselor can help them understand their options and make informed decisions.

Here's an example of a delinquency property tax notice:

Delinquency Notice

Texas Tax Assessor's Office

Address: 123 Main St, Austin, TX 78701

Phone: (512) 555-1212

Notice of Delinquent Property Tax

Property Location: 123 Oak Ave, Houston, TX 77056

Tax Account Number: 123456

Owner: John Doe

Dear John Doe,

This notice is to inform you that your property located at 123 Oak Ave, Houston, TX 77056, has delinquent property taxes owed *for the current year. The amount owed is $1,500.00, including penalties and interest, as of January 31, 2023.*

The taxes for this property are payable annually and become delinquent on January 31st of each year. According to the Texas Property Tax Code, if taxes are not paid within the prescribed time, interest and penalties will be added to the amount owed.

Please take immediate action to pay the delinquent taxes and avoid any further penalties. You may pay online at our website or by mail to the address above.

If the taxes remain unpaid, the property may be sold at a tax sale to satisfy the delinquent taxes. The sale of your property would result in the loss of ownership and any equity you have in the property.

If you have any questions or concerns, please do not hesitate to contact us at (512) 555-1212.

Sincerely,

Texas Tax Assessor's Office

The abovementioned Delinquency Notice is an example of an official document sent by the Texas Tax Assessor's Office to inform property owners of their delinquent property tax status. It provides information about the amount owed, including penalties and interest, and the consequences of non-payment, which could result in the loss of ownership and equity in the property. The notice advises property owners to take immediate action to pay the taxes and avoid any further penalties.

Avoiding Foreclosure for Reasons Beyond Tax Delinquencies: Exploring Alternative Options

When facing foreclosure, there are several options homeowners can explore to avoid losing their property. Reinstatement is the process of paying all the past-due payments and fees to bring the mortgage current. If the homeowner is unable to pay the full amount owed, they can look into partial reinstatement, where they pay a portion of the past-due amount to bring the mortgage current. Another option is to rent the property. This can provide a steady stream of income that can be used to pay the mortgage and prevent foreclosure.

In some cases, homeowners can also consider bankruptcy. This can provide a temporary stop to foreclosure proceedings and give the homeowner time to reorganize their finances. However, it is important to note that filing for bankruptcy has long-term implications, so it should only be considered a last resort.

Homeowners can also sign up for a forbearance agreement with their lender. This agreement temporarily suspends mortgage payments while the homeowner works to get back on track. Another option is to work out a loan modification with the lender, which may involve changing the terms of the mortgage to make the payments more affordable. Lastly, refinancing the property with a new mortgage can also help to lower monthly payments and avoid foreclosure.

It is crucial for homeowners to act quickly when facing foreclosure. If the property tax delinquency notice has been received, it is important to take immediate action and explore all available options to avoid losing the property. Reinstatement, renting the property, bankruptcy, forbearance, loan modification, and refinancing are just a few options that can be considered. However, each homeowner's situation is unique, and it is recommended to seek advice from a financial expert or an attorney to determine the best course of action.

(Note: Filing for bankruptcy should not be taken lightly, as it has long-term consequences that can affect a person's financial stability. While it may provide immediate relief from debt, it also has a negative impact on one's credit score, making it difficult to obtain loans or credit in the future. Moreover, bankruptcy remains on a person's credit report for up to 10 years, making it a visible blemish on their financial history. Additionally, certain assets, such as homes and vehicles, may be sold to repay creditors. It is important to consider all options before making the decision to file for bankruptcy and to work with a financial advisor or attorney to determine if it is the best course of action.)

Options for Homeowners Unable to Keep Their Homes: Strategies and Resources to Consider

If you're behind on your payments, the first step is to contact the creditor and attempt to negotiate a payment plan. Many creditors are willing to work with homeowners to find a solution that works for both parties. Negotiating a payment plan can help you get back on track and keep your home.

If you are unsuccessful with negotiations, refinancing your loan may help you lower your monthly mortgage payment and make it easier to keep your home. You may also be able to extend the term of your loan, which will also lower your monthly payment. Refinancing may not be an option for everyone, but it's worth considering if you're struggling to make your mortgage payments.

If you're facing a lien or foreclosure, seeking legal assistance as soon as possible is important. An attorney can review your case, help you understand your rights, and provide guidance on the best course of action to take. An attorney can also represent you in court and negotiate on your behalf with creditors.

If you're unable to keep your home due to a lien, it's important to understand your options and take action as soon as possible. Negotiating with the creditor, refinancing your loan, selling your home, and seeking legal assistance are all options to consider. The most important thing is to take action and seek help if you're struggling to keep up with your payments. Don't wait until it's too late to act, as this could result in losing your home to foreclosure.

Another option for someone who is unable to keep their home is a **short sale**. A short sale is a real estate transaction in which the homeowner sells their property for less than the outstanding mortgage balance. The sale proceeds are then used to pay off the outstanding mortgage debt. This type of transaction is becoming increasingly common in today's housing market. It offers a solution for homeowners who are facing financial difficulties and cannot keep up with their mortgage payments.

Short sales have been a part of the real estate market for many years, but their popularity increased during the housing crisis of the late 2000s. During this time, many homeowners faced foreclosure and could not sell their homes for enough to cover their outstanding mortgage debt. The short sale process allowed homeowners to sell their property and avoid the negative consequences of foreclosure, including damage to their credit score and the loss of their home.

To understand how a short sale works, let's walk through an example.

Suppose John and Sarah, who live in a home worth $200,000, have an outstanding mortgage balance of $225,000. Due to job loss and other financial difficulties, they can no longer keep up with their mortgage payments. To avoid foreclosure, they decide to pursue a short sale.

Contact the Lender.

To start the short sale process, the homeowner needs to contact their lender and explain their financial situation. In this case, John and Sarah would need to contact their lender and provide information on their financial difficulties. They would need to provide documents such as proof of income, tax returns, and bank statements to show they are experiencing financial hardship and cannot continue making mortgage payments.

Once the lender has reviewed their financial situation and determined that a short sale is viable, they will issue a short sale approval letter. This letter outlines the terms of the short sale, including the approved sale price and any conditions that need to be met before the sale can proceed.

Find a Real Estate Agent

After receiving approval from their lender to proceed with a short sale, John and Sarah will need to enlist the services of a real estate agent who is experienced in handling short sales. A specialized agent can provide valuable guidance and support throughout the process, which can be complex and time-consuming.

The agent will work with John and Sarah to list the property and market it to potential buyers. They may also assist in preparing necessary documents, such as a hardship letter explaining why a short sale is necessary and submitting the required paperwork to the lender.

It is important for John and Sarah to choose an agent who has a successful track record with short sales and who is knowledgeable about the local market. A skilled agent can help ensure that the property is priced appropriately and marketed effectively, increasing the chances of finding a qualified buyer and successfully completing the short sale.

Prepare and Submit a Short Sale Package

The short sale package is a crucial part of the short sale process that contains important financial information about the homeowner, including John and Sarah's income, assets, expenses, and debts. It also includes information about the property, such as its condition, location, and market value. The lender will use this information to determine whether or not to approve the short sale.

It's important to note that the short sale package must be carefully prepared and submitted in a timely manner to increase the chances of approval. A knowledgeable real estate agent can help homeowners prepare the necessary documents and ensure that they are submitted correctly to the lender.

The lender will carefully review the short sale package and

determine if it meets their specific criteria for a short sale. They will consider the homeowner's financial hardship, the current state of the real estate market, and the potential loss they may incur by accepting the short sale offer.

Overall, the short sale package is an important document that helps the lender assess the homeowner's financial situation and determine if a short sale is the best option for both parties.

Wait for Approval

After submitting the short sale package, John and Sarah will need to wait for the lender's decision. The waiting period can be stressful and may take several weeks or months. During this time, the lender will review the short sale package and determine if they are willing to accept the proposed sale price as payment in full for the outstanding mortgage balance. The lender may also request additional information or documents, further prolonging the process. It's important for John and Sarah to maintain communication with their lender and real estate agent during this time, as any delays or issues that arise must be promptly addressed.

If the lender approves the short sale, they will provide a short sale approval letter outlining the terms and conditions of the sale. This letter will typically include the approved sale price and any conditions that must be met before the sale can be completed. However, it's important to note that the lender may not approve the short sale even after all the necessary steps have been taken. If this happens, John and Sarah may need to consider other options, such as loan modification or bankruptcy.

Close the Sale

After the lender approves the short sale, the real estate agent will begin the process of finding a buyer for John and Sarah's property. This process can take some time, as the property must be marketed, and potential buyers must be found. Once a buyer has been identified, the real estate agent will work with the lender to finalize the terms of the sale.

At closing, the proceeds from the sale will be used to pay off the outstanding mortgage debt and any other fees or costs associated with the sale. It is important to note that in a short sale, the lender may forgive any remaining debt that is not covered by the sale proceeds, but this is not always the case.

Overall, a short sale can be a complicated and time-consuming process, but it can be a viable option for homeowners who are struggling to keep up with their mortgage payments and facing the possibility of foreclosure. Working with a knowledgeable real estate agent and seeking advice from a financial expert or attorney is important to navigate the process and understand the potential consequences.

Some individuals choose to avoid the short sale process by

choosing to submit the **Deed-in-Lieu of Foreclosure**. A Deed-in-Lieu of Foreclosure (DIL) is a real estate transaction in which the homeowner voluntarily transfers ownership of their property to the lender in order to avoid foreclosure. This type of transaction offers a solution for homeowners who are unable to keep up with their mortgage payments and want to avoid the negative consequences of foreclosure, including damage to their credit score and the loss of their homes.

Deed-in-Lieu of Foreclosure has been a part of the real estate market for many years, but its popularity increased during the housing crisis of the late 2000s. During this time, many homeowners were facing foreclosure and were looking for alternative solutions to avoid the negative consequences. The Deed-in-Lieu process allowed homeowners to transfer ownership of their property to the lender and avoid the negative consequences of a foreclosure.

Let's explore an example to understand how a Deed-in-Lieu of Foreclosure works.

Suppose John and Sarah, who live in a home worth $200,000, have an outstanding mortgage balance of $225,000. Due to job loss and other financial difficulties, they can no longer keep up with their mortgage payments. To avoid foreclosure, they decide to pursue a Deed-in-Lieu.

Step 1: Contact the Lender

The first step in this process is to contact the lender and inform them of the homeowner's financial situation. The lender may require the homeowner to provide documentation such as bank statements, pay stubs, and tax returns to verify their financial hardship. If the lender determines that the homeowner is eligible for a Deed-in-Lieu, they may ask the homeowner to provide a letter explaining why they cannot continue to make their mortgage payments and why a Deed-in-Lieu is the best option.

Step 2: Prepare and Submit a Deed-in-Lieu Package

In order to start the Deed-in-Lieu process, John and Sarah will need to provide the lender with a package of financial and property information. This package typically includes documentation such as tax returns, pay stubs, bank statements, and a hardship letter explaining the reasons for the request. The lender will use this information to determine if John and Sarah are eligible for a Deed-in-Lieu and whether it is in their best interest to accept the request. The lender will also review the property information to determine the current market value of the property and assess any outstanding liens or other encumbrances.

Step 3: Wait for Approval

After submitting the Deed-in-Lieu package, John and Sarah must wait for the lender's approval. The lender will review the package and consider several factors, such as the current market value of the property and the outstanding mortgage debt. This process can take several weeks or even months, and the lender may request additional information or documentation during this time.

It's important to note that the lender is not obligated to approve a Deed-in-Lieu request. They may require John and Sarah to first attempt to sell the property through a short sale or explore other options to avoid foreclosure. Additionally, the lender may require John and Sarah to vacate the property and leave it in good condition before the transfer of ownership is complete.

Step 4: Transfer Ownership

If the lender approves the Deed-in-Lieu request, John and Sarah will be required to sign over the property's title to the lender. This will transfer ownership of the property to the lender, an-uhd John and Sarah will no longer be responsible for the outstanding mortgage debt. However, it's important to note that a Deed-in-Lieu can have a negative impact on John and Sarah's credit score, similar to a foreclosure.

A Deed-in-Lieu of Foreclosure can be an effective solution for homeowners who are unable to keep up with their mortgage payments and want to avoid foreclosure. By transferring ownership of their property to the lender, homeowners can avoid the negative consequences of foreclosure and move on with their lives. The

Deed-in-Lieu process requires coordination between the homeowner and the lender, but with the right support, it can be a successful solution for those facing a difficult financial situation.

Understanding the Reasons Behind Property Tax Delinquencies: Why Some Property Owners Struggle to Pay

Property taxes are a crucial source of revenue for local governments and are used to fund various public services such as schools, roads, and public safety. Despite the importance of paying property taxes, many individuals and households fail to pay on time, leading to a wide range of consequences. Let's explore the various reasons why people fail to pay their property taxes and the impact it has on both individuals and communities as a whole.

Financial hardship is a major factor that contributes to property tax delinquencies. When individuals experience job loss, reduced income, or other financial difficulties, they may prioritize other bills over their property taxes. This is especially true when they are faced with pressing financial obligations like medical bills, rent or mortgage payments, or other debts. In some cases, homeowners may also struggle to pay their property taxes because of unexpected expenses, such as major home repairs or medical emergencies, that strain their finances. Additionally, some property owners may simply not understand the importance of paying their property taxes on time or may not have the necessary financial literacy to manage their finances effectively. Understanding the reasons behind property tax delinquencies can help local governments and property owners work together to find solutions to address the issue.

In some cases, individuals may be unaware that they are responsible for paying property taxes. This may occur if the individual is a recent homeowner or if they have not received clear communication from the local government regarding their tax obligations. The property tax payment process can be confusing and difficult to navigate, leading some individuals to miss payment deadlines or accidentally underpay their taxes. This may be due to a lack of understanding of the payment process or a failure to receive clear instructions from the local government. In some cases, individuals may dispute the amount they are required to pay in property taxes due to an inaccurate property assessment. This may lead to a delay in payment or a failure to pay the full amount owed.

When individuals fail to pay their property taxes on time, they may face serious financial consequences such as late fees, interest charges, and legal penalties. The risk of losing their property through a tax sale or foreclosure is also a concern. Moreover, their credit score can suffer, and it becomes harder to secure loans or other forms of credit in the future. Property tax delinquency impacts not only individuals but also the community at large as it reduces the amount of revenue available to fund essential public services such as schools, roads, and public safety.

Financial hardship is a common reason for individuals struggling to pay their property taxes, and other pressing financial obligations may cause property taxes to become a low priority. It is important for individuals to be aware of the consequences of property tax delinquency and to take necessary steps to address their financial situation and avoid delinquency.

Taking Action to Resolve Property Tax Issues: Strategies for Protecting Your Property and Financial Well-Being

Property taxes are a significant financial obligation for homeowners, and it's essential to understand the process of calculating, paying, and complying with these taxes. The calculation of property taxes is based on the assessed value of a property and the local tax rate. The local government determines the assessed value of a property and takes into consideration factors such as size and location, condition, and recent improvements. The local tax rate, determined by the local government, is then used to calculate the amount of property taxes owed.

Calculating property taxes can seem complex, but homeowners need to understand the process. In the following example, we will take a look at the calculation of property taxes for 123 Main Street, which has an assessed value of $300,000 and a taxable value equal to its corresponding market value. We will use an assessment rate of 35% and a local tax rate of 2% to illustrate the process of calculating property taxes. This example will provide a clear and concise explanation of the calculation and help to shed light on this important financial obligation:

$300,000 * 0.35 = $105,000

Next, the property tax can be calculated by multiplying the assessed value by the local tax rate of 2%:

$105,000 * 0.02 = $2,100

So, the property tax for 123 Main Street, assessed at $300,000 with a taxable value equal to its corresponding market value and a local tax rate of 2%, would be $2,100.

Property taxes can be paid in various ways, including through mail, online, or in person. Some local governments may also offer automatic payment options such as automatic debit or credit card payments for added convenience.

Property taxes are usually due in installments with payment periods and deadlines determined by the local government. Payment periods may be monthly, quarterly, or semi-annual, and deadlines may vary based on the local government. It is important to be aware of these payment periods and deadlines and to make payments on time to avoid late fees and penalties.

Failing to pay property taxes on time can result in severe financial penalties such as late fees, interest charges, and legal penalties. In some cases, individuals may even face the loss of their property through a tax sale or foreclosure. Hence, it is crucial to comply with payment deadlines and make timely payments to avoid these penalties.

In conclusion, paying property taxes is a significant financial obligation for homeowners, and understanding the calculation, payment, and compliance process is crucial. By being aware of these factors and making timely payments, individuals can avoid the financial penalties and consequences associated with failing to pay property taxes.

Chapter Four
Strategies for Resolving Property Tax Debt: Exploring Tax Lien Sales, Redemption, and More

Property taxes are a critical source of revenue for local governments, funding essential services like public schools, emergency services, and infrastructure improvements. As a property owner, it is your responsibility to stay on top of your property tax payments to avoid falling into debt or delinquency. However, sometimes unforeseen circumstances can make it difficult to keep up with these payments, resulting in tax liens or even the possibility of a tax lien sale.

In this chapter, we will explore the various options available for property owners who are facing tax debt or delinquent property taxes. We will start by discussing tax lien sales, which are public auctions where tax liens are sold to the highest bidder. These sales can be a stressful and overwhelming experience for property owners, but there are steps you can take to avoid them.

We will then dive into different strategies for resolving your property tax debt, including compromise, abatement, or deferral. A compromise is an agreement between the taxpayer and the local government to settle the debt for less than the full amount owed.

Abatement is the reduction or elimination of penalties or interest charges on the tax debt. Deferral allows taxpayers to delay paying their property taxes until a later date.

Lastly, we will discuss redemption, which is the process of paying off the tax lien to regain control of the property. This can be a complicated and time-consuming process, but it is often the best option for property owners who want to avoid losing their property to a tax lien sale.

Understanding your options and taking action early is key to solving your property tax debt or delinquent property taxes. By exploring the strategies, we cover in this chapter, you can take control of your financial situation and protect your property from tax liens or sales.

Delinquent property taxes are taxes that have not been paid by the due date. Property tax debt can accumulate quickly and can have serious consequences if left unresolved. In some states, if property taxes are not paid, the local government can place a lien on the property or even initiate foreclosure proceedings. Your property tax bill will list the amount of taxes owed, the due date, and the methods of payment. It is important to review your property tax bill carefully to ensure that you are aware of your financial obligation and the due date for payment.

If you are struggling to pay your property taxes, there are

several solutions available. One option is to enter into a payment plan with the local government. This plan will allow you to make smaller, more manageable payments over an extended period.

In order to be eligible for a repayment program, the homeowner must contact the local government and provide proof of their financial hardship. The local government may then work with the homeowner to create a payment plan that fits their budget. For example, John, a homeowner in Michigan, was unable to pay his property taxes on time due to a sudden loss of income. He contacted the local tax assessor's office and was able to enroll in a payment plan. Under the plan, John will make monthly payments over the next 12 months to resolve his delinquent property taxes.

Another option is to apply for a property tax exemption or credit, which can reduce the amount owed. In some cases, you may be able to negotiate a settlement with the local government to reduce the amount owed. In Tennessee, a homeowner, Sarah, struggled to pay her property taxes due to a recent medical emergency. She was able to apply for a property tax exemption, which reduced the amount owed based on her financial situation. However, even with the exemption, she could still not pay the full amount. Sarah then reached out to the local tax assessor's office to negotiate a settlement. After providing proof of her financial hardship, she was able to negotiate a reduced amount, which she was able to pay in full. Sarah could resolve her delinquent property taxes without losing her home.

It is important to be honest with your tax assessor about any financial hardships causing you to fall behind on paying your property taxes. This can be a difficult conversation to have, but it is crucial for finding a solution that works for both you and the local government. If you are experiencing financial hardship, it is in your best interest to reach out to the tax assessor as soon as possible. By being transparent about your situation, you may be able to negotiate a settlement or enroll in a payment plan that fits your budget. On the other hand, if you ignore the issue, you may face penalties, legal action, or even lose your home. Being honest and proactive can help you find a resolution and avoid further complications.

Showing good faith by making payments, even if they are small, can also demonstrate to the tax assessor that you are committed to resolving your delinquent property taxes. By making payments, you show that you are taking the matter seriously and are taking steps to address the issue. This can help build trust with the local government and increase the likelihood of finding a mutually beneficial solution. It is important to understand that every situation is different, and the tax assessor may have various options available to you based on your financial circumstances. Regardless of the situation, making payments and being honest about your financial hardship can go a long way in finding a resolution and avoiding further consequences.

Tax Lien Sales: What You Need to Know About the Process and Your Rights as a Property Owner

The history of tax lien sales dates back to the 1800s, when it was first used as a way for local governments to collect taxes from property owners who were unable or unwilling to pay. Over time, the process has evolved, and today, tax lien sales are typically managed through an auction process. During an auction, the local government will sell the tax lien to the highest bidder, who then has the right to collect the delinquent taxes from the homeowner. This process is used in many states across the country and is a crucial component of the local government's ability to fund essential services. In each state, there are different legal rights of investors and homeowners when it comes to tax sales.

For example, in some states, the local government will sell the tax lien to the highest bidder at a public auction, while in other states, the local government may offer the tax lien to private investors. In some counties, the homeowner has the right to redeem the tax lien within a certain timeframe, while in others, the tax lien becomes the property of the third-party investor.

Regardless of the state and county, the tax lien sale process typically begins with a notice of the sale being sent to the homeowner. The notice will include information about the amount owed, the date of the sale, and any other relevant details. If the homeowner fails to pay the delinquent taxes prior to the sale, the tax lien will be sold to the highest bidder.

Once the tax lien is sold, the new owner has the right to collect the delinquent taxes and any interest and penalties from the homeowner. The process of collecting delinquent taxes can vary and may include filing a lawsuit, foreclosing on the property, or negotiating a payment plan with the homeowner.

In most states, the sale is conducted through an auction in which the person willing to pay the most cash for the tax lien wins. This method is designed to ensure that the government is able to recover as much money as possible to cover the outstanding property tax debt. However, some states have adopted a bid-down process for their property tax lien sales. In this process, investors submit bids indicating how much interest they are willing to accept on their investment. The lowest bidder wins the auction, allowing the government to recover its property tax debt while also providing an opportunity for investors to earn a return on their investment. Regardless of the process used, the goal of a property tax lien sale is to recoup the outstanding property tax debt and prevent further delinquency.

As a winning bidder in a property tax lien sale, you have acquired the right to collect the delinquent property taxes the property owner owes. If the property owner pays the overdue taxes within the timeframe required by state law, you will receive your investment capital back, plus any interest earned. The interest rate for tax lien investments can be substantial, with many states setting a statutory rate between 10% and 12%.

For example, if you purchased a tax lien in Yuma County, Arizona, there is a specific process to ensure fairness and transparency. The bidding for the tax lien certificates begins at a set rate of sixteen percent (16%) and is awarded to the bidder who offers to accept the lowest rate of interest. To obtain a deed on the property, the winning bidder must file for judicial foreclosure of the tax lien in the Superior Court of Yuma County, where the property is located.

During the time that the winning bidder holds the tax lien certificate, the property is subject to redemption by the original owner. In the event of redemption, the winning bidder will receive the purchase amount minus non-refundable fees plus the rate of interest that was bid at the time of the sale, not exceeding 16%. This means that if a winning bidder bids at a lower interest rate, they may receive less in return if the property is redeemed.

For example, if a property owner owes $10,000 in unpaid property taxes and a winning bidder bids $15,000 at a 12% interest rate, and the property is redeemed after a year, the winning bidder would receive $15,000 plus 12% of the original $15,000, for a total of $16,800.

Cook County in Illinois is one of the largest counties in the United States, with a population of over 5 million people. The County Treasurer is responsible for conducting tax sales in Cook County, which typically occur sometime after the second installment of property taxes is due. During these tax sales, a "tax buyer" can purchase the overdue taxes and penalties owed by a property owner, thereby placing a lien on the property.

When a tax buyer in Cook County purchases a property's overdue taxes, they make a payment that is distributed among local taxing districts, such as schools and libraries. However, the property owner must still pay the tax buyer in order to regain a clear title to their property. The amount owed to the tax buyer consists of the delinquent tax, monthly interest, tax buyer interest, and various fees.

Tax buyers are able to charge very high-interest rates on their investments, as much as 36% per year. This high-interest rate makes it imperative for property owners to pay their overdue taxes as soon as possible, as failing to do so can result in the tax buyer eventually gaining ownership of the property.

Consider, for instance, a property owner in Cook County owes $10,000 in delinquent taxes and penalties. If the tax buyer purchases the overdue taxes and penalties at a 36% interest rate, the property owner would owe a total of $13,600 after one year. This amount would include the original delinquent taxes and penalties, as well as $3,600 in interest charged by the tax buyer. In Cook County, the tax sale process and the rights of property owners are governed by Illinois state law.

The redemption period is a crucial aspect of property tax sales that homeowners and investors need to understand. It varies from state to state and can have a significant impact on the outcome of the tax sale. In order to provide a comprehensive understanding of this topic, let's take a look at the redemption period in seven additional states:

1. **Florida**: In Dade County, Florida, the redemption period lasts for two years. During this time, the homeowner may redeem the property by paying the amount of taxes, penalties, and interest to the tax certificate holder. The interest rate for redemption in Dade County is 18% per annum.

2. **Tennessee**: In Shelby County, Tennessee, the redemption period lasts for one year. The interest rate for redemption in this county is a high rate, typically between 24% and 36% per annum.

3. **New York**: In New York County, the redemption period is set at two years. The interest rate for redemption in this county is also high, typically between 18% and 24% per

annum.

4. **Texas**: In Harris County, Texas, the redemption period lasts for two years. The interest rate for redemption in Harris County is 18% per annum.

5. **California**: In Los Angeles County, California, the redemption period is set at three years. The interest rate for redemption in this county is typically around 18% per annum.

6. **Georgia**: In Fulton County, Georgia, the redemption period lasts for two years. The interest rate for redemption in Fulton County is set at 18% per annum.

7. **Illinois**: In Cook County, Illinois, the redemption period is set at two years. The interest rate for redemption in Cook County is typically between 18% and 36% per annum.

It's important to note that the information provided above is subject to change and may vary based on the latest laws and regulations in each state. It's crucial for anyone interested in buying tax liens to research and understand the redemption period and interest rate in the specific county where they plan to invest.

The percentage of homeowners who redeem their delinquent property taxes within one year of a tax sale can vary greatly depending on the state and specific county. On average, about 30-

50% of homeowners redeem their property taxes within the redemption period, which typically ranges from 6 months to 2 years after the sale. To find out the exact redemption rate for a specific state or county, investors can research local tax sale information and statistics or contact the county's tax assessor's office.

The process of purchasing tax liens can be a lucrative investment opportunity for those who are interested in investing in real estate. In some states, once the redemption period has expired, the purchaser of a tax lien can gain title to the property. This can happen if the property owner fails to pay the delinquent property taxes, penalties, and interest within the designated timeframe. This process varies from state to state, but some examples include the following:

1. **New Jersey:** In New Jersey, the redemption period lasts for 18 months after the tax sale, and if not redeemed, the tax lien holder may obtain a tax deed.

2. **Georgia:** In Georgia, the redemption period lasts for 2 years after the date of the tax sale, and if not redeemed, the tax lien holder may obtain a tax deed.

3. **North Carolina:** In North Carolina, the redemption period lasts for 2 years after the date of the tax sale, and if not redeemed, the tax lien holder may obtain a tax deed.

4. **Virginia:** In Virginia, the redemption period lasts for 3 years

after the date of the tax sale, and if not redeemed, the tax lien holder may obtain a tax deed.

5. **Indiana:** In Indiana, the redemption period lasts for 2 years after the date of the tax sale, and if not redeemed, the tax lien holder may obtain a tax deed.

6. **Colorado:** In Colorado, the redemption period lasts for 2 years after the date of the tax sale, and if not redeemed, the tax lien holder may obtain a tax deed.

7. **Utah:** In Utah, the redemption period lasts for 2 years after the date of the tax sale, and if not redeemed, the tax lien holder may obtain a tax deed.

8. **Missouri:** In Missouri, the redemption period lasts for 1 year after the date of the tax sale, and if not redeemed, the tax lien holder may obtain a tax deed.

9. **Wisconsin:** In Wisconsin, the redemption period lasts for 1 year after the date of the tax sale, and if not redeemed, the tax lien holder may obtain a tax deed.

10. **Oregon:** In Oregon, the redemption period lasts for 2 years after the date of the tax sale, and if not redeemed, the tax lien holder may obtain a tax deed.

Investors need to understand the laws and regulations of the state in which they plan to purchase tax liens, including the redemption period, in order to make informed investment decisions. Also, it is important to do research in order to better understand the legal requirements in each state where you plan to invest in tax liens. This information can typically be found on the state's public website.

In many cases, when a property has a mortgage on it, it is less likely to go to a tax sale. This is because the lender will often pay the property taxes to ensure their lien remains intact and is not reduced through a tax sale. Most mortgage contracts contain a clause that allows the lender to add the advanced amounts for property taxes to the borrower's overall debt owed to the lender. This ensures that the lender's interest in the property is protected, even if the taxes go unpaid. Homeowners need to understand the terms of their mortgage contract and how it may impact their property in the event of delinquent taxes.

Preventing a Tax Sale: Tips and Strategies for Avoiding the Sale of Your Property Due to Unpaid Taxes

A tax sale can be a costly and time-consuming process for homeowners, leading to the loss of their property or additional debt. Fortunately, there are steps homeowners can take to avoid a tax sale and keep their property.

1. Stay on top of property tax payments: Make sure to pay property taxes on time, as the most common reason for a property going to tax sale is overdue taxes.

2. Monitor the amount owed: Keep track of the amount owed on property taxes, as additional fees and penalties can quickly accumulate. This information can typically be found on the county's tax collector's website.

3. Seek assistance: If you're facing financial hardship, there may be assistance programs available to help you pay your property taxes. Contact your local government or a housing agency for information on available programs.

4. Work with the lender: If you have a mortgage on your home, reach out to the lender and let them know about your situation. Many mortgage contracts contain a clause allowing the lender to advance amounts for property taxes, ensuring their lien isn't affected by a tax sale.

If a homeowner believes their tax assessment is incorrect or unjustified, they have the right to object and request a reduction in the amount. Typically, there are two options available to the homeowner. Firstly, the taxpayer can argue that the assessment exceeds the taxable value of the property. This means that they believe the assessed value is higher than the actual market value of the property. Secondly, the taxpayer can argue that the property has been assessed disproportionately. This means they believe the assessment is not in line with similar properties in the area and is unfairly high in comparison.

Objecting to a tax assessment and seeking a reduction in the amount can be complicated and requires an understanding of state and local law. This is why it is highly recommended that homeowners seeking to object to a tax assessment retain the services of an attorney.

An attorney can advise and educate the homeowner on state and local law, as well as the steps required to object to a tax assessment and seek a reduction in the amount. They can also assist in the preparation and filing of the necessary paperwork and represent the homeowner in court if necessary.

It is important to note that the process of objecting to a tax assessment and seeking a reduction in the amount is time-sensitive. Most states have a deadline for filing an objection, and it is crucial that homeowners act quickly to preserve their rights.

By taking the necessary steps, homeowners can avoid the stress and costs associated with a tax sale and keep their property. However, it's important to note that the specific requirements and procedures may vary by state and county, so it's crucial to familiarize yourself with the laws and regulations in your area.

Alternative Solutions for Property Tax Debt: Exploring Compromise, Abatement, and Deferral Options

When faced with delinquent property taxes, there are several additional options that may be available to homeowners. The first option is to reach a compromise with the tax authority. This can involve negotiating a payment plan or a reduction in the amount owed in exchange for the homeowner making timely payments going forward.

Another option is to request an abatement of the taxes. An abatement is a reduction in the amount of taxes owed based on the homeowner's financial hardship or other grounds specified by the tax authority.

Abatement programs aim to provide financial relief to homeowners who may struggle to pay their property taxes due to factors such as age, income, personal status, or disability. To request an abatement, the homeowner will typically need to provide documentation of their financial situation and make a case for why they are unable to pay the full amount of taxes owed.

Let's explore a few real-life examples of homeowners who have benefited from abatement programs.

- **Older Homeowners** - In several states, older homeowners may be eligible for a reduction in their property taxes. For example, in Pennsylvania, residents who are 65 years or older and have a household income of less than $35,000 may be eligible for a property tax rebate. In New York, the Enhanced STAR program provides a property tax break to senior citizens with incomes under $86,000.

- **Veterans** - Veterans who have served in the military may also be eligible for property tax reductions in some states. In California, for example, disabled veterans may be eligible for a property tax exemption of up to $150,000. In Texas, disabled veterans may be eligible for a property tax exemption on their primary residence if they receive a disability rating from the Veterans Administration.

- **Surviving Spouse of a Police Officer or Firefighter** - In some states, the surviving spouse of a police officer or firefighter who died in the line of duty may be eligible for a property tax reduction. For example, in Illinois, the surviving spouse of a police officer or firefighter who died in the line of duty may be eligible for a property tax exemption of up to $100,000.

It is important to note that these are just a few examples of the property tax reduction programs available in different states. The eligibility criteria, the amount of the reduction, and the application process may vary from state to state. Homeowners who believe they may be eligible for a property tax reduction should research their state's specific programs and contact their local property tax office for more information.

Property tax reduction programs provide a much-needed

financial relief to eligible homeowners who may struggle to pay their property taxes. By understanding the different programs available in their state, homeowners can take advantage of these programs and reduce their financial burden. Homeowners need to seek the advice of a tax professional or a lawyer if they have any questions or concerns regarding their property tax assessment.

Finally, a homeowner may be eligible for a deferral of their delinquent taxes. A deferral allows the homeowner to postpone paying the taxes, either until a later date or until they are able to sell the property. However, the homeowner will typically be required to pay interest on the deferred amount.

In some states, property tax abatement is not an option for homeowners who are delinquent in their tax payments. For example, in Pennsylvania, if a homeowner owes back taxes on a property, they must pay those taxes in full before they can apply for any kind of property tax relief program. In New Jersey, if a homeowner is behind on their property taxes, they must enter into a payment plan with their local government and make timely payments in order to be eligible for property tax relief programs.

In Ohio, property tax abatement is only available for current taxes, and a homeowner cannot receive an abatement for taxes that are delinquent. In Michigan, if a homeowner is in arrears on their property taxes, they may not be eligible for property tax abatement until they bring their account up-to-date.

Homeowners need to understand the laws in their state regarding property tax abatement and the eligibility requirements, especially if they are facing financial difficulties and are behind on their property tax payments. Failing to take advantage of available abatement programs or to seek help in resolving tax debt issues can result in the loss of the property through a tax sale.

Redemption: What It Means and How It Can Help You Save Your Property from Tax Foreclosure

Redemption is the act of a property owner paying the amount due to the owner of the tax lien in order to regain ownership of the property. As mentioned previously, if a property owner does not pay their delinquent property taxes, the government will often sell the tax lien to an investor.

In many states, there is a specific time period known as the redemption period, during which the property owner can still redeem the tax lien. The redemption period varies by state but typically lasts between six months to two years after the tax sale. During this time, the property owner can pay the amount owed to the tax lien owner and regain clear title to the property.

For example, in the state of Texas, the redemption period lasts for two years after the date of the tax sale. During this time, the property owner can redeem the tax lien by paying the amount owed, including the delinquent taxes, interest, and fees. In Kentucky, the redemption period lasts for one year after the date of the tax sale.

In the state of Illinois, the redemption period lasts for 22 months from the date of the tax sale. During this time, the property owner can pay the amount owed to the owner of the tax lien, which includes delinquent taxes, interest, penalties, and fees. If the property owner fails to redeem the tax lien within the 22-month redemption period, the owner of the tax lien may file a petition to foreclose on the property.

It is important to note that in some states, the redemption period may be shorter for commercial properties compared to residential properties. Additionally, the redemption period may be extended for certain circumstances, such as the property owner filing for bankruptcy.

In conclusion, property tax debt or delinquent property taxes can be a serious financial issue for property owners. However, solutions are available for those struggling with this type of debt. Understanding the different options, such as tax lien sales, compromise, abatement, deferral, and redemption, can help property owners take action to resolve their tax debt and avoid the risk of foreclosure or other legal consequences. It's important for property owners to be proactive and seek assistance from qualified professionals, such as tax attorneys or financial advisors, to find the best solution for their individual circumstances. With the right approach and guidance, property owners can overcome their tax debt and regain control of their financial situation.

Chapter Five

Exploring Your Options: Navigating Strategies for Dealing with Property Tax Liens

Dealing with a property tax lien can be a challenging and overwhelming experience for property owners. When faced with a tax lien, it's important to understand the options available for resolving the issue. In this chapter, we will explore various options for navigating a property tax lien, including contracting for a high-interest loan from a private lender, refinancing your loan, applying for a rescue loan, applying for a property tax deferral, filing for bankruptcy, selling the house to an investor, working out a payment plan, auctioning the home, and opting for a short sale.

For many property owners, a high-interest loan from a private lender is often the only option to resolve a property tax lien. However, other alternatives may be more feasible for some property owners. Applying for a property tax deferral is an option that allows property owners to postpone their tax payments until a later date, typically with interest. Filing for bankruptcy is another option that may provide relief from a property tax lien, but it can have significant long-term consequences. Selling the house to an investor, auctioning the home, and opting for a short sale are other options that may be suitable for property owners who are unable to keep up with their tax payments.

Each option has its own advantages and disadvantages, and it's essential to consider all available options carefully. In the following sections, we will explore the various options in more detail, including the potential risks and benefits associated with each. By understanding the options available, property owners can make informed decisions and choose the most appropriate solution for their unique circumstances.

It is important to take prompt action when facing delinquent property taxes. In some states, property tax abatement may not be possible if you are already delinquent in your tax payments. For example, in New York, property tax abatement is only available to individuals who have been paying their taxes in a timely manner. Suppose you have fallen behind on your property tax payments. In that case, you may not be eligible for the STAR (School Tax Relief) program, which reduces eligible homeowners' school property taxes.

Similarly, in Pennsylvania, individuals who are delinquent in their property tax payments may not be eligible for the Property Tax/Rent Rebate program, which provides rebates to eligible Pennsylvanians who are 65 years or older, widows and widowers 50 years or older, and those with disabilities. In Texas, individuals who are delinquent in their property tax payments may not be eligible for the Property Tax Deferral for the Elderly program, which allows eligible elderly taxpayers to defer all or part of their property taxes until their death, the sale of the property, or when they no longer reside in the property.

Therefore, staying informed and understanding your state's laws is crucial. The local government's website or tax office is a good place to start for information on payment options and deadlines.

When property taxes go unpaid for three years, the county is likely to take action to collect the delinquent taxes through a process called foreclosure. The first step in this process is the announcement of the foreclosure, which will be sent via mail, posted on the homeowner's door, or delivered in person. This notice will inform the homeowner of the county's intention to foreclose on the property if the delinquent taxes are not paid.

States like Washington, Oregon, and Idaho have strict laws regarding property tax delinquency and have implemented strict penalties and fees for homeowners who fall behind on their property tax payments. An administrative fee will augment the standard penalties for delinquent taxes in these states if the homeowners want to begin making payments as part of a plan to pay off the debt, as well as the redemption fee. If the property taxes remain unpaid for more than three years, the county may move to foreclose on the property to recoup the delinquent taxes. Foreclosure proceedings are typically announced through a notice, which can be sent via mail, posted on the property door, or delivered in person. The notice will inform the homeowner of the county's intent to foreclose and the steps they need to take to redeem the property and avoid foreclosure.

In a previous section, it was suggested to consult with a tax collector or attorney to identify the steps that can be taken to resolve a property tax debt. The following chapter provides a brief overview of some of these options. It is highly recommended to seek professional assistance, as it can greatly aid in finding a resolution to the debt.

Using High-Interest Loans from Private Lenders to Resolve Property Tax Debt: Understanding the Risks and Benefits

When faced with a property tax lien, many homeowners may feel overwhelmed and uncertain about how to address their debt. One option to consider is obtaining a high-interest-rate loan from a private lender. While this option may seem like an easy solution, it is important to weigh the pros and cons before making a decision. A high-interest rate private loan may cause further financial hardship for the homeowner. One example of how these types of loans can contribute to financial hardship is when a homeowner on a fixed income obtains borrow money with an interest rate of 20%.

If the homeowner takes out a loan to pay off a $10,000 tax lien and chooses to pay the loan off over a period of 5 years, the homeowner will end up paying over $15,000, including $5,000 in interest fees. This high-interest cost can create a significant financial burden for the homeowner and may make it difficult for them to keep up with other financial responsibilities. While this option can provide quick and easy access to funds, it has its own advantages and disadvantages. Consider the following pros and cons of high-interest-rate private loans:

Pros:

1. Quick Access to Funds: Private lenders often offer fast loan approvals and can provide the funds needed to pay off the tax lien within a short period of time. This can be especially helpful if the homeowner needs to address the lien quickly in order to avoid a tax sale or foreclosure.

2. No Impact on Credit Score: Unlike other forms of borrowing, a loan from a private lender is not reported to credit bureaus and will not affect the homeowner's credit score.

Cons:

1. High-Interest Rates: Private lenders often charge higher interest rates than traditional banks or lending institutions. This can lead to an increase in the overall debt owed and make it more difficult to pay off the loan in the long run.

2. Risk of Foreclosure: If the homeowner is unable to repay the loan, the private lender may foreclose on the property. This can lead to the loss of the home and the addition of a foreclosure on the homeowner's credit report.

3. Limited Loan Options: Private lenders often have limited loan options and may only offer loans for a specific purpose, such as paying off a tax lien. This can limit the homeowner's ability to find a loan that meets their needs and financial situation.

It is important to thoroughly research private lending options and consider seeking the advice of a financial advisor before making a decision. In some cases, a loan from a private lender may be a viable option for homeowners facing a tax lien. However, it is crucial to consider all of the potential consequences and weigh the pros and cons before making a final decision.

Refinancing Your Loan to Resolve Property Tax Debt: Understanding Your Options and the Process

For many homeowners facing a tax lien, refinancing their loan may seem like a daunting task. However, this option can be a valuable solution for those who are struggling to keep up with their property tax payments and are looking for a way to resolve their debt. Refinancing a loan essentially means taking out a new loan with a different lender to pay off the original loan. The homeowner may be able to secure a lower interest rate, longer repayment term, or both, which can make it easier to manage their monthly payments.

The benefits of refinancing your loan to address a tax lien include the following:

1. Lower monthly payments: By securing a lower interest rate, homeowners may be able to reduce the amount they need to pay each month.

2. Longer repayment term: With a longer repayment term, homeowners may be able to spread out the amount they need to pay over a longer period of time, making it easier to manage.

3. Consolidate debt: Refinancing can be a way to consolidate multiple debts into one monthly payment, making it easier to keep track of and manage.

The drawbacks of refinancing your loan to address a tax lien include the following:

1. Closing costs: Refinancing a loan typically involves paying closing costs, which can be a significant upfront expense.

2. Credit score impact: Refinancing a loan can impact a homeowner's credit score, especially if they have a low credit score or have recently taken out multiple loans.

3. Long-term commitment: Refinancing a loan can involve

committing to a long-term repayment plan, which may not be feasible for some homeowners.

It's important for homeowners to carefully consider the pros and cons of refinancing their loan for a tax lien and to work with a financial advisor to determine the best course of action. Some real-life examples of homeowners who have successfully refinanced their loan to address a tax lien include:

Example 1: Sarah, a homeowner in Washington, had fallen behind on her property tax payments and was facing a tax lien. She refinanced her loan and was able to secure a lower interest rate and longer repayment term. This allowed her to reduce her monthly payments and regain control of her finances.

Example 2: John, a homeowner in Oregon, had multiple debts, including a tax lien, that he was struggling to manage. He decided to refinance his loan and was able to consolidate all of his debts into one monthly payment. This made it easier for him to keep track of his finances and helped him get back on track.

In conclusion, refinancing a loan can be a valuable solution for homeowners facing a tax lien. However, it's important to consider the pros and cons and to work with a financial advisor to determine the best course of action.

Applying for a Rescue Loan to Address Property Tax

Debt: Understanding the Requirements and Benefits

A rescue loan is a type of loan designed to provide financial assistance to individuals or property owners facing difficult financial situations, such as tax liens. This type of loan was created to provide a solution for those who are struggling to pay their property taxes and face the risk of losing their property. The purpose of a rescue loan is to help individuals overcome their financial hardship, pay off their tax debts, and keep their property. The origin of rescue loans can be traced back to the early 2000s, when the housing market faced challenges, and homeowners struggled to keep up with their mortgage and property tax payments.

Advantages of Obtaining a Rescue Loan:

1. Immediate Relief: One of the main benefits of a rescue loan is that it provides immediate relief from a tax lien. You can use the loan to pay off the delinquent taxes, which will lift the lien from your property.

2. Avoid Foreclosure: If the tax lien on your property remains unpaid for a period of time, the county may move to foreclose on your property. A rescue loan can help you avoid foreclosure by providing the funds you need to pay off the delinquent taxes.

3. More Time to Pay Off Debt: A rescue loan can give you more time to pay off delinquent taxes without having to

worry about the threat of foreclosure. This can help you resolve your financial difficulties in a more manageable and stress-free way.

Disadvantages of Obtaining a Rescue Loan:

1. High-Interest Rates: One of the main drawbacks of a rescue loan is that it often comes with high-interest rates. This means that you will end up paying more in interest over the life of the loan, which can make it difficult to get out of debt.

2. Short Repayment Period: Another drawback of a rescue loan is that it often has a short repayment period. This means you will need to repay the loan quickly, which can be difficult if you are already struggling with your finances.

A rescue loan can be another viable option for homeowners who are facing a tax lien.

Information on rescue loans and options that can be used to avoid foreclosures can be obtained through a HUD-certified counseling agency. HUD counseling agencies started as a response to the increasing number of homeowners struggling with debt and the need for impartial and expert advice. The US Department of Housing and Urban Development (HUD) recognized this need and established a network of certified counseling agencies to help homeowners navigate the complex financial landscape and find solutions to their problems. These agencies offer a wide range of services, including housing counseling, financial management, and debt management, and are staffed by trained and experienced professionals who are committed to helping homeowners achieve their financial goals. Over the years, HUD-certified counseling agencies have helped millions of homeowners overcome financial difficulties and achieve financial stability.

The services provided by a HUD-certified counseling agency typically come at no or low cost to the homeowner. The agency may charge a fee for their services. However, this fee is often nominal and may be waived for low-income individuals. It is important to note that while the agency may not charge a fee, they may require payment of third-party fees, such as an appraisal or credit report fees. It is important to check with the specific agency for their fee structure and any associated costs before utilizing their services.

Rescue Loans for Property Tax Debt: When High-Interest Loans Are the Only Option

If you're facing a tax lien on your property, you may be considering a high-interest loan as an option to pay off your debt. However, it's important to take several factors into consideration before making a decision. One of the first things to consider is the interest rate. In California, for example, high-interest loans for tax liens can have an interest rate of 15% or higher. This means that you could end up paying significantly more in interest than the original amount of your tax debt. In the state of New York, the government places a cap on high-interest rates. This means lenders are not allowed to charge an interest rate above a certain percentage set by the state. The exact cap varies depending on the type of loan and the borrower's creditworthiness, but the maximum rate is generally around 16% for consumer loans. Some states with high caps include South Dakota, which allows an interest rate of 36%, and Oklahoma, which allows an interest rate of 16%. It's important to note that these caps apply to various types of loans, not just those related to personal loans and may also be subject to change.

Another factor to consider is the terms of the loan. In Arizona, some lenders may require that you pay off the loan within a year, while others may allow you to make payments over several years. The difference in paying off a $10,000 loan in one year versus five years with a 15% interest rate can be substantial. With a one-year loan, the monthly payment would be higher, but the overall interest paid would be lower. On the other hand, with a five-year loan, the monthly payment would be lower, but the total interest paid over the life of the loan would be higher. For example, a one-year loan with a 15% interest rate would require a monthly payment of $966.67 and result in an interest payment of $1,500. In contrast, a five-year loan with the same interest rate would require a monthly payment of $219.05 and result in an interest payment of $3,390. It is important to consider both the monthly payment amount and the total interest paid when deciding on the length of a loan to pay off a tax lien. Make sure you understand the terms of the loan before you agree to it so you know what you're signing up for.

In addition to the interest rate and terms of the loan, you should also consider the fees associated with the loan. In Utah, for example, some lenders may charge a loan origination fee, which can add several hundred dollars to the cost of the loan.

Finally, it's important to think about your long-term financial stability. In Oregon, for example, taking out a high-interest loan to pay off a tax lien could put a strain on your finances for several years to come. The state recognizes that taking out a high-interest loan can have a negative impact on a person's financial stability in the long term. By putting a cap on the interest rate, Oregon is ensuring that consumers are not overburdened by loan repayment and can maintain a stable financial situation. Make sure you understand the long-term implications of the loan before you agree to it.

Taking out a high-interest loan to pay off a tax lien can be a good option in some circumstances, but it's important to consider all of the factors involved before making a decision. Make sure you understand the interest rate, terms of the loan, fees, and long-term implications before you agree to it. If you're unsure of what to do, consider speaking with a financial advisor or a HUD-certified counseling agency for guidance.

Property Tax Deferral: Exploring Your Options and How to Apply for Relief

For some homeowners, a property tax deferral may provide a much-needed solution to their financial difficulties. A property tax deferral is a government-sponsored program that allows eligible homeowners to defer paying their property taxes for a specified period of time.

The eligibility requirements for a property tax deferral vary from state to state, but they typically involve being at least 60 years of age, disabled, or having a low income. In addition, the applicant must occupy the property as their primary residence and must not have defaulted on any previous tax deferral agreements. It is important to note, however, that not all states provide this option, and the terms and requirements may vary from state to state.

For example, in Washington, property owners who are over the age of 61 or who are disabled can apply for a property tax deferral. In Oregon, property owners can apply for a deferral if they are over the age of 55 or are disabled, while in Idaho, property owners must be over the age of 65 to be eligible for a deferral. In each of these states, the property owner must meet certain income requirements to be eligible for a deferral, and the amount of taxes deferred will accrue interest until they are paid.

One of the major benefits of a property tax deferral is that it can help you avoid the costs and stress of a tax lien or foreclosure. Furthermore, a property tax deferral provides you with the time you need to get back on your feet and regain your financial stability.

Applying for a property tax deferral is relatively straightforward. Generally, you will need to complete an application, provide proof of income and residency, and possibly attend an in-person interview.

Filing for Bankruptcy to Resolve Property Tax Debt: Understanding Your Options and the Consequences

Filing for bankruptcy is a drastic measure that can have long-lasting impacts on a homeowner's financial stability. However, it may be an option for those facing a property tax lien, especially if they are unable to pay their debts through other means. The bankruptcy process typically involves a filing with the U.S. Bankruptcy Court, which will then oversee the process. In some cases, the court may require the homeowner to attend a meeting with their creditors to negotiate a payment plan. The outcome of this process will depend on the homeowner's specific financial situation, including the amount of debt they owe and their income.

One of the main impacts of filing for bankruptcy is that it will negatively affect the homeowner's credit score. This will make it difficult for the homeowner to obtain credit in the future, including loans for a car, home, or education. Additionally, filing for bankruptcy may result in the homeowner losing some of their assets, including property and personal belongings, to repay their debts.

Another impact of filing for bankruptcy is that it will be reflected on the homeowner's credit report for up to 10 years. This will make it difficult for them to obtain credit during this time. However, they may be able to obtain credit from lenders who specialize in working with individuals with a bankruptcy on their records.

Selling Your Property to an Investor to Resolve Property Tax Debt: Understanding the Pros and Cons of this Option

Selling a home to an investor allows homeowners the opportunity to pay off the outstanding tax debt, as well as any other outstanding debts or bills, by transferring ownership of the property. While this option may seem like a quick solution, it's important to understand the process and the potential impact on the homeowner before making a decision.

The process of selling a house to an investor typically involves reaching out to a real estate agent who can help find a suitable investor who is interested in purchasing the property. Real estate investors generally look for properties with a good return on investment potential. This may include properties that are undervalued and in need of repairs, properties in desirable locations with good rental income potential, and properties with the potential for future appreciation. Additionally, real estate investors also consider the market conditions and competition in the area, as well as the zoning regulations and any other factors that may affect the value of the property.

Once the sale is complete, the homeowner will be relieved of their tax debt, as well as any other outstanding debts or bills. However, there are also potential drawbacks to this option. Selling the house to an investor often results in a loss of equity, which means that the homeowner may receive less money than they would have if they had sold the property on the open market. Additionally, the homeowner may have to give up control over the property, which can be difficult for some people. It is also possible that the investor may ask the homeowner to sign a lease agreement, which can further limit the homeowner's control over the property.

Another impact of selling the house to an investor is that the homeowner may not be able to qualify for a new mortgage for several years after the sale, which can further limit their financial options.

One of the most common ways real estate investors find properties with tax liens is by searching public records. This information is publicly available and can be found at the county or state level, depending on the property's location.

Tax liens are considered public records because they represent a claim by the government on a property for unpaid taxes. This information is typically recorded with the county or state and is accessible to anyone searching for it.

There are several ways that real estate investors can access this information, including online searches, visiting the county recorder's office, or contacting a title company. Some states also have a central database where tax liens are recorded and searchable by the public.

It is important to note that while tax liens are public records, the process for accessing this information can vary greatly depending on the state or county. Some states have more robust public record systems, while others may have limited information available.

Negotiating a Payment Plan to Resolve Property Tax Debt: Strategies and Tips for Success

Working out a payment plan with the tax collector or government agency responsible for collecting the taxes can be a mutually beneficial solution for both the homeowner and the government. The homeowner is able to repay their debt in a manageable way, and the government is able to receive the funds owed to them.

The process of working out a payment plan can vary depending on the state or local government but typically involves contacting the tax collector or government agency responsible for collecting the taxes and explaining your financial situation. You may need to provide documentation of your income, expenses, and assets in order to negotiate a payment plan that works for both parties.

It is important to note that the terms of a payment plan may not be flexible, and it is important, to be honest with the tax collector or government agency about your financial situation in order to avoid defaulting on the payment plan and facing additional penalties. Additionally, the payment plan may come with additional fees or interest, so it is important to understand the full terms and costs of the plan before entering into it.

The desired end result of working out a payment plan for a tax lien is for the homeowner to successfully repay their debt in a manageable way and for the government to receive the funds owed to them. This can help the homeowner avoid additional penalties or legal action, and it can help to improve their overall financial situation by resolving the tax lien.

Auctioning Your Home to Resolve Property Tax Debt: Understanding the Process and Your Rights as a Property Owner

Auctioning the home should be a last resort option for homeowners facing a tax lien. In this scenario, the government may sell the property to the highest bidder in order to recoup the owed taxes. This can be a difficult and stressful process for the homeowner, who may lose the property they have lived in and invested in for years.

The process of auctioning the home typically starts when the government posts a notice of the sale in a local newspaper and on the property. The homeowner then has a set amount of time to pay the owed taxes or negotiate a payment plan. If the taxes are not paid, the government will proceed with the auction.

In some states, the auction is conducted by the local government and is held at the property. The highest bidder at the auction will then take ownership of the property, subject to the tax lien. In other states, the auction may be conducted online, with bidders bidding from all over the country.

Before the auction can take place, the homeowner is typically notified of the delinquent taxes and given a chance to pay the amount owed. If the taxes are not paid, the property is then listed for auction. The auction itself can take anywhere from a few days to several months to complete, depending on the size and complexity of the property, as well as the bidding process. Some states may also have a minimum bid requirement, which can further impact the length of time it takes to complete the auction.

When a property is put up for auction due to a property tax lien, the homeowner may be responsible for paying certain fees to the auctioneer. These fees can include administrative fees, marketing costs, and commissions. In New York, an auctioneer may charge a fee of 10% of the sale price of the property to handle the auction. In Texas, the fee can be as low as 5%, while in California, the fee may be a flat rate of $500. Homeowners need to be aware of these fees when considering an auction as an option for addressing a property tax lien, as they can reduce the amount of money the homeowner is able to recoup from the sale of their property.

One of the biggest disadvantages of auctioning the home is that the homeowner is likely to receive much less for the property than its actual market value. This is because the government is looking to recoup the owed taxes, not to maximize the sale price. Additionally, the homeowner will have no control over who buys the property and may be forced to move out quickly.

Choosing a Short Sale to Resolve Property Tax Debt: Understanding the Process and Requirements

The short sale process involves negotiating with the lender

to accept a sale of the property for less than the amount owed on the mortgage. This process can be a difficult and lengthy one, requiring the homeowner to work closely with their lender and real estate agent. The length of time it takes to complete a short sale can vary depending on the complexity of the situation and the lender's requirements, but it typically takes several months from start to finish.

There are several key elements that must be in place to get a short sale approved. First, the homeowner must demonstrate that they are unable to pay their mortgage, either due to financial hardship, unemployment, or other factors. This may require providing documentation such as pay stubs, bank statements, and other financial records.

Next, the homeowner must work with their mortgage lender to determine the market value of the property and negotiate a sale price that is lower than the outstanding mortgage balance. This typically involves submitting a detailed hardship letter, explaining the circumstances that led to the homeowner's financial distress, and presenting a detailed financial plan for how they will manage their finances in the future.

The mortgage lender must then review the homeowner's documentation and approve the short sale. This process can take several weeks or even months, depending on the lender's internal processes and the complexity of the homeowner's financial situation.

Once the short sale is approved, the homeowner must find a buyer for their property and close the sale. The sale proceeds are then used to pay off the outstanding mortgage balance, and any remaining funds are returned to the homeowner.

In terms of impact on the homeowner, a short sale can have both positive and negative consequences. On the one hand, it can provide a way to resolve the property tax lien and avoid foreclosure. On the other hand, it will likely have a negative impact on the homeowner's credit score and may impact their ability to secure future financing. Additionally, the homeowner will have to vacate the property, which can be a difficult process, emotionally and logistically.

Finding a Path Forward: Navigating Your Options for Addressing a Property Tax Lien

When faced with a property tax lien, homeowners have several options available to them. One option is to contract for a high-interest loan from a private lender. This may be seen as a last resort, as the high-interest rate can put a strain on the homeowner's finances for years to come. Another option is to refinance their loan, if possible, in order to better manage their monthly payments.

For those who need immediate relief, an option to consider is applying for a rescue loan. This loan is specifically designed to help homeowners who are struggling with their mortgage and property tax payments. However, it's important to understand that this type of loan often comes with high-interest rates, making it an option that should be considered with caution.

For homeowners who would like to keep their homes, a property tax deferral may be a better option. This allows homeowners to defer their property tax payments for a certain period of time, giving them a chance to catch up on their finances. Another option is filing for bankruptcy, which can provide a fresh start for homeowners struggling to make their mortgage and tax payments.

Those who would like to sell their home have the option of selling it to an investor. This is often a quick solution, as investors are looking to buy homes at a discount and are often willing to pay cash. However, this option may impact the homeowner's credit score and could result in a lower sale price than what they may have received on the open market.

Homeowners also have the option of trying to work out a payment plan with their local government. This option can provide a manageable solution, as it allows homeowners to pay off their tax debt in smaller, more manageable payments. If a payment plan is not an option, homeowners may need to consider auctioning their homes. This is a quick solution, as the auction process can be completed within a few months.

Finally, opting for a short sale may be an option for homeowners who are facing a property tax lien. A short sale is when the homeowner sells their home for less than what they owe on their mortgage and property tax debt. This option can provide a solution for homeowners who are struggling to make their payments and want to avoid foreclosure. It's important to understand that a short sale can impact the homeowner's credit score and may take several months to complete.

In conclusion, dealing with a property tax lien can be a daunting task for any homeowner. However, by understanding the various options available, they can navigate through the process and find a solution that works for their specific situation. It is important to consider all options carefully, weighing the pros and cons of each approach before making a decision. While a high-interest loan from a private lender may seem like the only option for some, it is crucial to explore other possibilities, such as refinancing or applying for a rescue loan. Additionally, filing for bankruptcy, selling the house to an investor, or auctioning the home are all viable options that should be considered. Homeowners can also opt for a property tax deferral or work out a payment plan with the local government. Lastly, opting for a short sale may be a better alternative to foreclosure. Regardless of the option chosen, it is essential to take action as soon as possible to avoid further damage to their credit score and financial situation.

Furthermore, one valuable resource is a HUD-certified counseling agency. These agencies are staffed by knowledgeable professionals who can help you understand your rights and responsibilities, as well as provide you with personalized guidance and support. By consulting with a HUD-certified counseling agency, you can gain a better understanding of the options available to you and take steps to address your tax lien in a way that is manageable and sustainable for you.

Chapter Six

Selling Your Home with a Lien: Navigating IRS Certificates, Releases, and Priority

When it comes to selling a home with a lien, property owners may encounter various obstacles that can make the process challenging. A lien is a legal claim against a property that gives the creditor or lien holder the right to take action to collect the debt if it is not repaid. If a lien is not addressed before attempting to sell a property, it can hinder the sale and create a difficult situation for both the seller and buyer.

In this chapter, we will explore the options and steps involved in selling a home with a lien. One important aspect of addressing a lien is obtaining an IRS certificate of release or a release of lien or discharge of property. This document indicates that the lien has been satisfied and allows for the property to be sold without any legal complications.

Additionally, there are other options that property owners can explore, such as subordination or withdrawal of the lien. Lien priority is also an important factor to consider, as it determines the order in which liens are paid off in the event of a sale.

Navigating the complexities of liens and selling a property requires specialized expertise and knowledge of the legal system. It is crucial for property owners to seek professional guidance and assistance to ensure a successful and smooth sale.

In the following sections of this chapter, we will delve into the details of each option for selling a home with a lien, including the pros and cons of each approach. By understanding the various options and potential obstacles, property owners can make informed decisions and successfully sell their property with a lien.

When faced with outstanding debts or property taxes, some homeowners may choose to use the equity in their homes to pay off their financial obligations. Two main options for leveraging home equity are re-mortgaging the home or selling the property. Re-mortgaging, also known as refinancing, involves drawing down equity in the home to access additional capital for servicing debt. This essentially means exchanging ownership in the house for the elimination of liabilities such as personal loans, credit card debt, or delinquent taxes.

Refinancing a mortgage can provide homeowners with the funds needed to pay off debts. This is a useful approach for those with multiple smaller debts, like high-interest credit card balances, as consolidating them into one loan can result in a lower monthly payment with a significantly smaller interest rate. This approach offers a more manageable cash flow than dealing with many unpaid loans at once. To get the best deal, homeowners should approach several different lenders and compare offers before making a decision.

Selling the home is the second option, and it has its own set of advantages. One significant benefit of selling a home to pay off debts is the intangible sense of financial freedom that comes with being debt-free. However, it's important to note that the seller will need to make alternate living arrangements. If the seller can make these arrangements before their credit rating is severely impacted, they may still be able to purchase a new home, even if they're selling their current one to clear debts.

It's important to note that if there is a federal tax lien on your home, you must satisfy the lien before you can sell or refinance the property. This is according to information available on the official website of the Internal Revenue Service (IRS.gov).

However, there are several options available to satisfy the tax lien. For instance, you may pay off the outstanding tax debt and any associated interest and penalties in full to remove the lien. Alternatively, you may qualify for a lien release if you can demonstrate that the lien is impairing your ability to sell the property or if the IRS determines that releasing the lien won't jeopardize your ability to collect the debt.

The IRS increased its threshold for tax liens in 2011 due to inflationary pressures and a struggling economy. Prior to this, the agency could impose a tax lien on an individual's property, assets, or bank accounts for debts as low as $5,000. However, this threshold was raised to $10,000, meaning that if you owe less than this amount, the IRS may be willing to work out an overdue tax installment payment plan with your tax attorney. It's important to note that you must still pay your taxes or risk facing significant penalties, including the possibility of jail time.

Fortunately, the IRS also instituted a policy that works to the benefit of taxpayers. At the same time, it increased its threshold for tax liens. If you owe more than $10,000 in back taxes and are faced with a lien on your property, you can formally request that the IRS withdraw the lien once your bill has been paid in full. This is a valuable option to keep in mind when dealing with tax liens and can help alleviate the stress and financial burden associated with such situations.

If you are able to pay off the back taxes in full and request the withdrawal of the tax lien from the IRS, they will erase any record of the lien from public records. This is a significant benefit for homeowners looking to sell their property, as the lien will no longer impact their credit score. However, it's important to note that it may take some time for the IRS to remove the lien from public records and for credit reporting agencies to update their records accordingly.

When you have a lien on your property, it can significantly reduce your credit score by several hundred points. Credit reporting agencies view a tax lien as a serious red flag, and it will remain on your credit reports for up to seven years, even after it has been paid off unless you actively file for an IRS withdrawal.

When selling a property with a tax lien, the lien will typically be paid out of the sales proceeds at the time of closing, in part or in full, depending on the amount of equity in the property. If the sale proceeds are not enough to cover the lien amount, the taxpayer may request that the IRS discharge the lien to allow for the completion of the sale. It's crucial to work with an experienced real estate broker who can guide you through this process and ensure that the lien is resolved appropriately, allowing you to sell your property without any issues.

When dealing with a federal tax lien, taxpayers or lenders can ask the IRS to make the lien secondary to a lending institution's lien. This can be helpful for those who want to refinance or restructure their mortgage and need the lien removed to do so. In 2018, the IRS worked to expedite requests for discharge or mortgage restructuring to assist taxpayers in these situations.

In 2018, the IRS reviewed the results and impact of their increased dollar thresholds for when liens are generally filed. The increase was made to better assist struggling taxpayers and align with inflationary changes since the last revision. The review found that the new threshold was effective in helping more taxpayers avoid having a tax lien placed on their property, reducing the number of liens filed by over one-third in the first year alone. This positive outcome made it easier for taxpayers to avoid the negative impact that a tax lien can have on their credit score and financial situation. Overall, the increased dollar threshold has been a success in helping taxpayers who are struggling with past-due balances.

While tax liens can be a significant financial burden, the IRS has policies and procedures in place to assist taxpayers in resolving their tax debt and avoiding the negative consequences of a lien. Two of the most important options available to taxpayers are Direct Debit Installment Agreements (DDIAs) and lien withdrawals.

DDIAs allow taxpayers to make monthly installment payments through an automatic debit from their bank account. With a DDIA, taxpayers can pay off their tax debt over time and avoid having a tax lien filed against their property. To be eligible for a DDIA, taxpayers must owe $50,000 or less in combined individual income tax, penalties, and interest. Additionally, taxpayers must be current on all tax filings and not have any outstanding prior tax debt. By entering into a DDIA, taxpayers can avoid the negative impact of a tax lien on their credit score and financial situation.

A lien withdrawal removes the public notice of the lien and

restores the taxpayer's credit score. The IRS will grant a lien withdrawal if the taxpayer meets certain criteria, including:

- The tax debt has been satisfied in full.

- The taxpayer has made three consecutive payments under a DDIA.

- The taxpayer can demonstrate that a lien withdrawal is in the best interest of the taxpayer and the government.

To request a lien withdrawal, taxpayers must submit Form 12277, Application for Withdrawal. The IRS will review the request and make a determination based on the taxpayer's circumstances. If the request is approved, the IRS will notify the credit reporting agencies to remove the lien from the taxpayer's credit report.

While tax liens can be a significant financial burden, the IRS has policies and procedures in place to assist taxpayers in resolving their tax debt and avoiding the negative consequences of a lien. By entering into a DDIA or requesting a lien withdrawal, taxpayers can avoid the negative impact on their credit score and financial situation. It's essential to understand the IRS policies and procedures and work with a knowledgeable tax attorney or real estate broker to ensure that you're making informed decisions when dealing with tax liens.

IRS Certificate of Release: What It Is and How It Can Help You Resolve Property Tax Debt

Taxpayers who have satisfied their tax liability or have had the lien released can take steps to remove the lien from their credit report and regain their financial freedom.

Section 6325(a) of the Internal Revenue Code directs the IRS to release a federal tax lien within 30 days of when the liability is fully paid or becomes legally unenforceable, or the IRS accepts a bond for payment of the liability. Once the taxpayer has satisfied the tax liability, the IRS will issue a Certificate of Release of Federal Tax Lien for filing in the same location where the notice of lien was filed.

This certificate is proof that the lien has been released, and the taxpayer is no longer obligated to pay the tax debt.

If the IRS has not released the lien within 30 days, the taxpayer can request a Certificate of Release. The request must be made in writing, and the taxpayer must provide proof that the tax liability has been satisfied or is legally unenforceable. Once the request is received, the IRS will review the taxpayer's account and determine if the release is warranted. If so, the IRS will issue the Certificate of Release of Federal Tax Lien.

Once the tax lien has been released, taxpayers can take steps to remove the lien from their credit report. To do this, the taxpayer must contact the credit reporting agencies and provide a copy of the Certificate of Release of Federal Tax Lien. The credit reporting agencies will then remove the lien from the taxpayer's credit report, which can have a positive impact on their credit score and financial situation.

It is essential to note that if the taxpayer does not obtain a Certificate of Release of Federal Tax Lien, the lien will remain on their credit report for up to seven years. This can significantly impact the taxpayer's ability to obtain credit, purchase a home, or take out a loan.

In conclusion, tax liens can be a significant financial burden on taxpayers who owe back taxes to the government. However, the IRS has procedures in place for releasing a tax lien once the liability is fully paid or becomes legally unenforceable. Once the lien is released, taxpayers can take steps to remove the lien from their credit report and improve their credit score and financial situation. Understanding the IRS policies and procedures and working with a knowledgeable tax attorney can help taxpayers make informed decisions and regain their financial freedom.

If a taxpayer has an immediate or urgent need for a Certificate of Release of Federal Tax Lien, they can visit or call their local IRS office. The IRS office can provide the taxpayer with the necessary documentation to obtain the Certificate of Release, and they can also provide guidance on how to satisfy the tax liability or become legally unenforceable.

Taxpayers can find a list of local IRS offices, their available services, and their hours of operation on the IRS website at www.irs.gov under "Local Contacts." It's essential to note that not all IRS offices provide the same services, so taxpayers should call ahead to confirm that the office they plan to visit can assist with their specific needs.

In addition to the financial benefits, obtaining a Certificate of Release of Federal Tax Lien can provide peace of mind for taxpayers who have been burdened by the lien. The process of satisfying a tax liability and obtaining a Certificate of Release can be stressful and time-consuming, but taxpayers need to take the necessary steps to regain their financial freedom and move forward.

Release of Lien or Discharge of Property: Understanding Your Options for Resolving Property Tax Debt

There are options available to have the lien removed from a specific property through a discharge. A discharge removes the lien from a specific property, freeing it from the government's legal claim.

There are several provisions in the Internal Revenue Code

(IRC) that determine eligibility for a discharge of property. Taxpayers can refer to IRS Publication 783, "Instructions on How to Apply for a Certificate of Discharge from Federal Tax Lien," for more details on these provisions.

In general, a taxpayer may be eligible for a discharge of property if they meet the following criteria:

- The taxpayer has sold the property, and the proceeds from the sale will be used to satisfy the tax liability.

- The property is not needed as collateral to secure the tax liability.

- The discharge will not hinder the government's ability to collect the tax liability.

Taxpayers must submit an application for discharge of property to the IRS. The application must include detailed information about the property and the proposed use of the proceeds from the sale. The IRS will review the application and make a determination based on the taxpayer's circumstances.

After the IRS reviews the petition, a letter of commitment will be issued, provided that the applicant meets the criteria for discharge. Under Internal Revenue Code (IRC) section 6325(b)(2)(B), if the IRS determines that there is no equity in the property, it will issue Pattern Letter P-402 or P-403. Pattern Letter

P-403 is issued when the IRS determines that its interest in the property is worth a specific dollar amount, while Pattern Letter P-402 is issued when its interest in the property is valueless. It's important to note that the amount of the IRS' interest in the property will be calculated based on the balances due on all encumbrances recorded ahead of the IRS' lien, including prior mortgages, unpaid taxes, and other relevant fees.

For example, suppose a taxpayer owes $50,000 in federal taxes and has a federal tax lien against their property, which has a market value of $200,000. The taxpayer applies for discharge of the tax lien, and the IRS reviews the petition, determining that the balances due on prior encumbrances, including the first and second mortgages, real estate taxes, and closing costs, total $190,000. After subtracting the prior encumbrances from the property value, the IRS determines that there is only $10,000 of equity in the property. Therefore, the IRS issues Pattern Letter P-403 under IRC section 6325(b)(2)(A), indicating that its interest in the property is worth $10,000.

The IRS determines the equity in the property by establishing the balances due on all encumbrances recorded ahead of the IRS' lien until the day of closing. This typically includes the first and second mortgage, any unpaid real estate taxes, and any judicial liens, regardless of whether there has been a tax sale.

To determine the equity, the taxpayer will need to provide a payoff statement from each creditor holding a lien on the property. The payoff statement will show the outstanding balance due on the lien, including principal, interest, and any other charges.

Once the outstanding balances have been established, the total amount is subtracted from the property's fair market value to determine the equity in the property. The equity is the amount that will be available to satisfy the tax liability, and the remaining balance will be discharged.

In addition to the outstanding balances on encumbrances, the equity determination should also include the closing costs associated with the sale of the property. Closing costs may include loan origination fees, points, agent's commissions, attorney's fees, and fees for recording all relevant information. These costs are subtracted from the equity to determine the net proceeds available to satisfy the tax liability.

A disagreement may arise as to what exactly constitutes a "prior encumbrance" when determining the equity available to satisfy the tax liability. The Internal Revenue Code (IRC) provisions that determine eligibility for a discharge of a federal tax lien refer to prior encumbrances recorded ahead of the IRS' lien. This typically includes the first and second mortgage, any unpaid real estate taxes, and any judicial liens.

However, other debts may also be considered prior encumbrances if they have a higher priority than the IRS lien. For example, if the property is subject to an outstanding judgment, that judgment would have a higher priority than the IRS lien and would be considered a prior encumbrance.

In some cases, disagreements may arise as to whether a particular debt constitutes a prior encumbrance. This is where working with a knowledgeable tax attorney can be beneficial in navigating the process and ensuring that all prior encumbrances are accurately identified.

Disagreements may also arise when determining the closing costs associated with a discharge. Closing costs may include loan origination fees, points, agent's commissions, attorney's fees, and fees for recording all relevant information. These costs are subtracted from the equity to determine the net proceeds available to satisfy the tax liability.

The IRS has specific guidelines on allowable closing costs, and disagreements may arise if the closing costs exceed these guidelines. For example, while the IRS will frequently allow 6-7% agent's commissions, it won't allow more than $750 in attorney's fees, regardless of the complexity of the transaction or the amount of work done by the attorney.

Let's say a taxpayer is applying for a discharge of a federal tax lien on a property with a fair market value of $500,000. The taxpayer owes $150,000 in back taxes and has outstanding balances on a first and second mortgage, unpaid real estate taxes, and a judgment lien.

The taxpayer works with their tax attorney to obtain payoff statements from each creditor holding a lien on the property. The outstanding balances on the liens total $400,000, leaving $100,000 in equity to satisfy the tax liability.

The attorney also identifies the allowable closing costs, including loan origination fees, agent's commissions, and attorney's fees. The closing costs total $25,000, leaving net proceeds of $75,000 available to satisfy the tax liability.

However, a disagreement arises as to whether the attorney's fees should be limited to $750. The attorney argues that the complexity of the transaction warrants a higher fee, while the IRS contends that the fee exceeds the allowable amount.

In this scenario, the taxpayer may need to work with their attorney and the IRS to resolve the disagreement and accurately determine the net proceeds available to satisfy the tax liability.

It's important to note that not all costs associated with the sale of the property may be included in the equity determination. For example, repairs or renovations to the property are typically not included in the determination.

A discharge of property can have several benefits for taxpayers. It allows them to sell the property without the burden of a federal tax lien, freeing them from the government's legal claim. The proceeds from the sale can then be used to satisfy the tax liability, potentially avoiding further penalties or interest.

In addition, a discharge of property can have a positive impact on a taxpayer's credit score and financial situation. Once the lien is removed from the property, it will no longer be a public record and will not affect the taxpayer's credit report.

Subordination.

When a taxpayer has a federal tax lien against their property and is looking to refinance or sell the property, they may encounter issues with their lender or buyer due to the lien. In these situations, subordination can be a useful tool for the taxpayer.

Subordination involves reordering the priority of liens on a property. With a subordination agreement, the IRS agrees to subordinate its lien to another lien, such as a mortgage or other financing, thereby allowing the lender or buyer to take first priority in the event of a foreclosure or other sale. Subordination can make it easier for a taxpayer to sell or refinance their property, as it allows them to work with their lender or buyer to ensure that the other party's interests are protected while still satisfying the federal tax lien.

To request subordination, the taxpayer must submit a written request to the IRS and provide documentation of the proposed transaction. The IRS will review the request and determine whether subordination is appropriate. The IRS may require additional information or documentation before making a decision.

It's important to note that subordination does not discharge the federal tax lien; it only reorders the priority of the lien. The taxpayer is still responsible for paying off the tax debt, and the lien will remain in place until the debt is satisfied.

For example, suppose a taxpayer owes $50,000 in federal taxes and has a federal tax lien against their property, which has a market value of $200,000. The taxpayer wants to refinance their mortgage to take advantage of lower interest rates, but the lender is unwilling to approve the loan because the federal tax lien has priority over their mortgage. The taxpayer submits a request for subordination to the IRS, along with documentation of the proposed refinance. After reviewing the request, the IRS determines that subordination is appropriate and agrees to subordinate its lien to the new mortgage. The taxpayer is able to refinance their mortgage and take advantage of lower interest rates while the IRS maintains its interest in the property, and the taxpayer remains responsible for paying off the tax debt.

Withdrawal

A withdrawal of a federal tax lien removes the lien from public records and releases the taxpayer's property from the lien's claims. This can be a useful tool for taxpayers who want to sell or refinance their property, as it removes the lien's negative impact on their credit score and financial situation.

To be eligible for a withdrawal of a federal tax lien, the taxpayer must meet certain criteria, including:

1. The tax debt must be paid in full, or the taxpayer must have entered into a Direct Debit Installment Agreement and made at least three consecutive payments.

2. The taxpayer must be in compliance with all current and prior tax filings.

3. The taxpayer must not have had any federal tax liens filed against them in the past three years.

4. The withdrawal is in the best interest of both the taxpayer and the government.

To request a withdrawal of a federal tax lien, the taxpayer must complete Form 12277, Application for Withdrawal, and provide supporting documentation to the IRS. The IRS will review the request and make a determination based on the taxpayer's circumstances. If the request is approved, the IRS will notify the credit reporting agencies to remove the lien from the taxpayer's credit report.

There are two types of withdrawals: the withdrawal of the Notice of Federal Tax Lien and the withdrawal of the Notice of Lien in Error. The withdrawal of the Notice of Federal Tax Lien removes the lien from public records and releases the taxpayer's property from the lien's claims. The withdrawal of the Notice of Lien in Error corrects an error in filing the lien.

It's important to note that a withdrawal of a federal tax lien does not discharge the tax debt. The taxpayer is still responsible for paying off the debt, but the withdrawal removes the negative impact of the lien on their credit score and financial situation.

For example, suppose a taxpayer owes $20,000 in federal taxes and has a federal tax lien against their property, which has a market value of $150,000. The taxpayer wants to sell the property and use the proceeds to pay off the tax debt, but the lien is preventing them from finding a buyer. The taxpayer meets the criteria for a withdrawal of the federal tax lien and submits a request to the IRS, along with supporting documentation. After reviewing the request, the IRS determines that a withdrawal is appropriate and approves the request. The lien is removed from public records, and the taxpayer is able to sell the property and use the proceeds to pay off the tax debt. The withdrawal also removes the negative impact of the lien on the taxpayer's credit score and financial situation.

Lien Priority: Understanding the Order in Which Liens Are Paid and How It Affects Your Property

When it comes to liens, priority refers to the order in which different creditors will be paid if a property is sold or foreclosed. The order of priority is crucial as it determines which creditor is entitled to the proceeds from the sale of the property. The general rule is that liens are paid in the order in which they were recorded. The first recorded lien takes precedence over all subsequent liens.

There are two types of liens: voluntary and involuntary. A voluntary lien is created when a property owner agrees to use their property as collateral for a loan. Examples of voluntary liens include mortgages and home equity loans. On the other hand, an involuntary lien is created without the property owner's consent. Examples of involuntary liens include tax liens and mechanics' liens.

The order of priority for liens is generally determined by the date on which they are recorded. The first lien to be recorded is the first in priority, while subsequent liens are subordinate to the first lien. For example, if a homeowner takes out a mortgage on their property, the mortgage is the first lien on the property. If the homeowner then takes out a home equity loan, the home equity loan is subordinate to the mortgage. In the event of a foreclosure, the mortgage lender will be paid before the home equity lender.

While the general rule is that liens are paid in the order in which they were recorded, there are some exceptions. One exception is for tax liens. Federal tax liens take priority over all other liens, regardless of when they were recorded. This means that even if a mortgage was recorded before a federal tax lien, the federal tax lien takes priority.

Another exception is for mechanics' liens. Mechanics' liens take priority over all other liens except for tax liens. This means that if a contractor files a mechanics' lien on a property, they will be paid before any other creditor, except for the IRS.

Understanding lien priority is crucial for both property owners and creditors. Property owners need to be aware of the order in which liens will be paid if their property is sold or foreclosed, while creditors need to be aware of their position in the lien priority hierarchy. While the general rule is that liens are paid in the order in which they were recorded, there are exceptions, such as federal tax liens and mechanics' liens, which take priority over other liens. Working with a knowledgeable real estate broker or tax attorney is essential to understand the priority of liens on your property.

The Importance of Specialized Expertise in Dealing with Property Tax Liens

Selling a home with a tax lien can be a complex and challenging process. As such, it often requires specialized expertise to ensure a successful transaction. Various experts, including tax attorneys, real estate brokers, accountants, and title companies, can provide valuable assistance throughout the process. The roles and responsibilities of each of these experts and the value they can bring to selling a home with a tax lien are often invaluable.

A tax attorney is a legal expert specializing in tax law. When selling a home with a tax lien, a tax attorney can provide essential guidance to ensure that the transaction is legally sound and compliant with IRS regulations. They can also help navigate any disputes or disagreements that may arise during the process. Their main responsibilities include:

1. Reviewing the tax lien and ensuring its validity.

2. Advising on options for satisfying the tax lien, such as installment agreements, offers in compromise, or filing for a lien discharge or subordination.

3. Ensuring all necessary paperwork and documents are in order, such as lien withdrawals or certificates of discharge.

4. Reviewing the purchase agreement and ensuring compliance with state and federal tax laws.

Real estate brokers are licensed professionals who help buyers and sellers with property transactions. When selling a home with a tax lien, a real estate broker can help market the property and find a buyer. They can also advise on pricing and negotiating with potential buyers. Their main responsibilities include:

1. Assessing the value of the property and determining a competitive selling price.

2. Marketing the property to potential buyers through various channels, such as online listings and open houses.

3. Finding a buyer and negotiating the terms of the sale, including addressing any tax lien issues that may arise.

4. Ensuring that all necessary documentation is in order, such as title reports and lien releases.

An accountant is a financial professional who can assist with tax planning and preparation. When selling a home with a tax lien, an accountant can provide essential guidance on the tax implications of the transaction. They can also help navigate any tax-related issues that may arise. Their main responsibilities include:

1. Assessing the tax implications of the sale, such as any capital gains taxes that may be owed.

2. Advising on strategies for minimizing tax liabilities, such as tax credits or deductions.

3. Preparing any necessary tax documents, such as Form 1099-S.

4. Ensuring compliance with federal and state tax laws.

A title company is a third-party agency that handles the closing process for a property sale. When selling a home with a tax lien, a title company can provide essential assistance in ensuring the transaction is legally sound and compliant with state and federal regulations. Their main responsibilities include:

1. Conducting a title search to ensure there are no liens or other claims against the property.

2. Preparing the closing documents and ensuring compliance with state and federal laws.

3. Handling the escrow process and ensuring all necessary funds are transferred to the appropriate parties.

4. Issuing a title insurance policy to protect against any future claims or disputes.

In conclusion, selling a home with a lien can be a complicated process. However, there are options available for homeowners to resolve the lien and sell their property. It's important to seek the expertise of professionals who can guide you through the process and help you understand your options. The IRS Certificate of Release, the release of lien or discharge of property, subordination, and withdrawal are all potential solutions to consider. Additionally, understanding lien priority and the potential impact on the sale of your home is critical. Don't hesitate to reach out to specialized experts for help in navigating this process and finding a solution that works for you. Selling your home with a lien may seem overwhelming, but it can be done successfully with the right support.

Chapter Seven

Selling Your Home Due to Delinquent Taxes: Tips and Strategies for Success

Selling your home due to delinquent taxes can be a stressful and overwhelming process. It's important to have a solid understanding of the steps involved in the sale and to have a reliable real estate agent on your side. In this chapter, we will explore tips for selling your home when you have delinquent taxes, with a particular focus on the role of a good real estate agent in the process.

A good real estate agent can make all the difference when it comes to selling a home with delinquent taxes. They can provide valuable guidance and support throughout the process, helping you navigate the complexities of the sale and ensuring that you get the best possible outcome.

In this chapter, we will discuss the qualities to look for in a real estate agent when selling a home with delinquent taxes. We will also cover the various steps involved in the sale, from preparing your home for listing to negotiating with potential buyers. Additionally, we will provide tips on maximizing the value of your home and minimizing the impact of delinquent taxes on the sale.

By working with a knowledgeable and experienced real estate agent, you can ensure that your home sale goes smoothly and that you get the best possible outcome. Whether you're looking to sell quickly or are willing to wait for the right buyer, the guidance and support of a good real estate agent can make all the difference. So, let's dive into the tips for selling your home due to delinquent taxes with the help of a reliable real estate agent.

Selling a home due to delinquent taxes can be a stressful experience. However, there are ways to make the process smoother and more successful. One of the most important tips is to work with a real estate agent who specializes in selling homes with liens or delinquent taxes. These professionals have the expertise to handle the complex legal and financial aspects of the sale and can provide you with valuable guidance and support.

When it comes to advertising your home, you need to reach a large audience in order to attract potential buyers. Your real estate agent can help you craft an effective advertising strategy that targets the right demographic. This may include listing your home in local newspapers, magazines, and real estate websites. The goal is to create a sense of urgency and competition among buyers.

An exemplary successful advertising campaign was done for a luxury home located in the hills of Los Angeles. The real estate agent partnered with a high-end lifestyle magazine and featured the property in a multi-page spread. The ad showcased the stunning views from the property, the luxurious interior design, and the extensive amenities such as a pool, spa, and outdoor entertainment area. Additionally, the agent hosted a VIP open house event, inviting potential buyers and luxury lifestyle influencers to experience the property firsthand. This combination of print advertising and exclusive event marketing resulted in a successful sale at a premium price.

This shows that the internet should be used to your advantage. The vast majority of home buyers start their search online, so it's important to have a strong online presence. Make sure your home is listed on all major real estate websites, such as Zillow, Realtor.com, and Redfin. Consider creating a virtual tour or video walkthrough to give buyers a more immersive experience. One example of a successful way in which the internet was used to sell a house is through virtual open houses. During the COVID-19 pandemic, many real estate agents began hosting virtual open houses through video conferencing platforms like Zoom or Facebook Live. This allowed potential buyers to view the property and ask questions in real time without having to physically visit the home.

One particularly successful example is a virtual open house hosted by a real estate agent in California. The agent created a video tour of the property, including a 3D walk-through, and hosted a live Q&A session on Facebook Live. The open house was advertised on social media platforms and targeted potential buyers in the area. The virtual open house was a hit, with hundreds of viewers tuning in and several serious inquiries from potential buyers. The house sold shortly after the event, proving the effectiveness of using the internet and technology to sell a property.

There are advantages to informing your neighbors that you are selling your home. Word of mouth is a powerful marketing tool; your neighbors can help spread the word to potential buyers. If your neighbors have friends or family members who are interested in buying a house in the area, they can spread the word to them. This is exactly what happened in a neighborhood in Virginia, where a homeowner put up a "for sale" sign in their yard and told their neighbors about the listing. One of their neighbors had a friend looking to buy a house in the area and could purchase the home quickly without the need for a real estate agent or marketing expenses. In addition to referrals, neighbors may also be able to help with the sale by keeping an eye on the property and alerting you to any issues or potential buyers they notice.

Another useful tip is to provide incentives to potential buyers. Incentives can motivate buyers to take action, especially if they are on the fence about making an offer. Incentives can often make a difference when it comes to selling a home, and there are many creative ways to entice potential buyers. One example of a successful incentive involved a seller offering to cover the cost of a one-year home warranty. This not only provided peace of mind to the buyer but also showcased the seller's commitment to ensuring the property was in good condition. The buyer was more willing to purchase the property, as they felt that the seller was willing to go the extra mile to ensure their satisfaction. Other examples of incentives might include covering closing costs, offering a furniture allowance, or providing a home improvement credit. It's essential to consider what incentives would be most valuable to potential buyers and work with a real estate agent to determine the most effective way to offer them.

Professional photos can make a huge difference in attracting potential buyers. You want your home to look its best, and professional photos can showcase its best features. According to a study conducted by Redfin, homes with professional photographs sold for an average of $3,400 to $11,200 more than homes without professional photos. The study also found that homes with professional photos were more likely to sell within six months than homes with amateur photos. Additionally, the study revealed that homes with professional photos received 61% more online views than homes with amateur photos. These statistics show the significant impact that professional photos can have on the sale of a home. Your real estate agent can recommend a photographer who specializes in real estate photography.

Social media can be a powerful tool in marketing your home to potential buyers. Your agent can create a social media campaign that targets potential buyers in your area. By leveraging social media platforms such as Facebook, Instagram, and Twitter, you can reach a wider audience of potential buyers and showcase your property in a visually appealing way.

Some tips for a successful social media campaign include:

1. Use high-quality photos and videos to showcase the best features of your home.

2. Use targeted advertising to reach the right audience. For example, you may want to target people in your local area who are currently looking to buy a home.

3. Utilize hashtags to increase the visibility of your posts. Consider using hashtags such as #forsale, #realestate, and #newhome.

4. Engage with your audience by responding to comments and messages in a timely manner.

5. Leverage user-generated content by encouraging potential buyers to share photos and videos of your property on their own social media profiles.

Proper landscaping can significantly enhance a property's aesthetic appeal and perceived value. According to the National Association of Realtors, investing in landscaping can result in a return on investment of up to 215%. A well-manicured lawn and garden can create a welcoming and inviting atmosphere that immediately impresses potential buyers.

To maximize the impact of landscaping on the sale of a home, it is essential to hire a professional landscaper with experience in preparing homes for sale. They can provide expert advice on the best landscaping designs for the property and recommend features that add value, such as outdoor lighting or a patio.

Some of the best tips for enhancing a home's landscaping include planting flowers and shrubs that complement the architectural style of the house, creating a well-defined garden path, and keeping the lawn neatly trimmed and weed-free. The landscaper can also recommend the most appropriate type of mulch to use and advise on adding outdoor water features or installing sprinkler systems.

Ultimately, professional landscaping can make a significant difference in the curb appeal of a home, attracting more potential buyers and leading to a faster sale at a higher price.

A video walk-through is an excellent way to provide potential buyers with an immersive experience of your property. You can create a video walkthrough highlighting the best features of your home and showcasing the property's layout. This can be a powerful tool in attracting buyers and closing a sale.

Selling a home with delinquent taxes can be a challenging

process, but by following the right tips and strategies, you can successfully sell your property and achieve financial stability. Working with a real estate professional, using the internet, advertising, informing your neighbors, providing incentives, professional photos, social media campaigns, landscaping, and video walkthroughs are some of the most effective ways to sell your home. By following these tips, you can ensure a successful sale and a brighter financial future.

The Role of a Good Real Estate Agent in Resolving Property Tax Debt: Tips and Strategies for Success

When trying to sell a property with a lien, it's important to use a good real estate agent who has experience dealing with such situations. Here are some tips on what to look for in an agent and what to avoid.

1. Look for an agent who has experience dealing with liens: A good agent should have experience dealing with liens and the process of releasing them. They should be able to guide you through the process and help you avoid any pitfalls.

2. Check their credentials: Make sure the agent you choose is licensed and has a good reputation in the industry. You can check their credentials online or by asking for references.

3. Look for an agent with good communication skills: A good

agent should keep you informed throughout the entire process and be able to explain everything in plain language. They should be able to answer any questions you have and be available when you need them.

4. Avoid agents who promise to solve your lien problems: It's important to remember that an agent cannot make the lien go away. They can only help you navigate the process of releasing it. Be wary of agents who promise to solve all your problems, as this is often too good to be true.

5. Look for an agent who is a good negotiator: When dealing with liens, it's often necessary to negotiate with the lien holder. A good agent should have strong negotiation skills and be able to work with the lien holder to find a solution that works for everyone.

6. Avoid agents who pressure you into making a decision: Selling a property with a lien on it can be a stressful and emotional process. Avoid agents who pressure you into making a decision before you're ready. A good agent should be patient and work with you to find the best solution for your needs.

7. Look for an agent who is familiar with your local market: A good agent should have a deep understanding of the local market and be able to advise you on pricing and marketing

strategies that are best suited to your property.

Once you have found a good real estate agent, it's essential to take advantage of their resources and expertise to market and sell your property efficiently, especially when dealing with a tax lien. The following are some options your agent can use to market your property:

1. Install a Highly Visible Yard Sign: The sign should include the agent's contact information to allow potential buyers to get in touch easily. The sign should be clear and attractive, and the agent should ensure that it's always clean and well-maintained.

2. Use Print Advertisement: Print advertising can be an effective marketing strategy when selling a property with a tax lien. Your agent should use local newspapers, real estate magazines, and other publications to advertise your property. These ads should contain high-quality images of your property, relevant details, and the agent's contact information.

3. Use Brochures: A well-designed brochure can help showcase your property's best features and provide potential buyers with a clear understanding of its layout and design. Your agent should create brochures that contain high-quality images, detailed descriptions, and the agent's contact

information. The brochures can be handed out during open houses or given to potential buyers who express interest in your property.

4. Arrange an Open House: An open house is an excellent opportunity for potential buyers to see your property, ask questions, and get a sense of the property's value. Your agent should advertise the open house to potential buyers through email marketing, social media, and other marketing channels. During the open house, the agent should be available to answer questions and provide additional information about your property.

Your agent can also provide other valuable insights, marketing strategies, and negotiating skills to help you sell your property quickly and for the best possible price.

Selling a home is a complex process involving several factors, including the home's physical appearance. Making small changes to your home's appearance can greatly impact its overall attractiveness to potential buyers. Here are some tips to consider when preparing your home for sale:

1. Gender Neutralization: To ensure your home appeals to as wide an audience as possible, it's essential to make it as gender-neutral as possible. This includes removing items such as overly masculine or feminine decor, colors, or

accessories. For example, a room that has traditionally been decorated in shades of pink should be repainted in a more neutral color.

2. Make the Kitchen More Attractive: The kitchen is often the heart of the home, and a well-designed and attractive kitchen can make all the difference when selling a home. Consider updating the kitchen with new appliances, countertops, or cabinetry. Simple changes such as replacing the hardware on cabinets or repainting the walls can also have a big impact.

3. Shelter Your Pets: It is important to remember that not all potential buyers will be animal lovers. When preparing your home for sale, removing any signs of pets, including pet beds, litter boxes, and food dishes, is a better approach. If possible, consider boarding your pets during open houses or showings.

4. Hire a Stager: A professional stager can be an excellent resource for preparing your home for sale. A stager can help you rearrange furniture, add decorative accents, and create a welcoming atmosphere that will appeal to potential buyers. Staging is particularly useful for currently empty homes, as it can help prospective buyers visualize the home's potential.

5. Clean the Home: A clean and tidy home is crucial when selling a property. Be sure to remove any clutter and thoroughly clean the property before showing it. This

includes deep-cleaning carpets, scrubbing bathrooms and kitchens, and dusting all surfaces. Hiring a professional cleaning service can be an excellent investment when selling a home.

In summary, making small changes to the physical appearance of your home can have a big impact on its overall attractiveness to potential buyers. Gender neutralization, updating the kitchen, sheltering your pets, hiring a stager, and thoroughly cleaning the home are all effective ways to prepare your home for sale. By following these tips, you can increase your home's appeal and potentially receive more offers from interested buyers.

Here are some additional ideas that could be considered when selling a home:

1. Consider making upgrades or repairs: In some cases, making upgrades or repairs to your home can increase its value and make it more attractive to potential buyers. This might include things like updating appliances, repainting, or replacing outdated fixtures.

2. Set a realistic price: Setting the right price is crucial when selling your home. Overpricing can lead to your home sitting on the market for too long while underpricing can result in lost profits. Consider working with a real estate agent to determine the right price for your home based on market

trends and other factors.

3. Be flexible with showings: Buyers may want to see your home at different times of the day or on weekends. Try to be as flexible as possible with showing times to accommodate potential buyers.

4. Keep your home clean and clutter-free: A clean and tidy home is more attractive to potential buyers. Be sure to keep your home clean and clutter-free, especially during showings or open houses.

5. Be prepared for negotiations: Buyers may try to negotiate the price of your home or request repairs or other concessions. Be prepared to negotiate and work with your real estate agent to come up with a strategy for handling negotiations.

Selling a home with a tax lien can be a daunting task, but it's not impossible. By working with a specialized real estate agent, you can navigate the legal and financial complexities of the sale and achieve a successful outcome. Advertising your home effectively, utilizing the internet, and informing your neighbors are some of the strategies that can help attract potential buyers. Strategies such as professional photos and proper landscaping can also enhance the appeal of your property. As discussed earlier, gender-neutralization, making the kitchen more attractive, sheltering your pets, hiring a stager, and keeping your home clean and clutter-free can make your home more appealing to potential buyers.

Other important tips to consider include making upgrades or repairs to your home, setting a realistic price, being flexible with showing times, and being prepared for negotiations.

In short, selling a home due to delinquent taxes can be a challenging and overwhelming experience. However, with the right approach and the help of a good real estate agent, it is possible to navigate this process successfully. By following the tips outlined in this chapter, property owners can increase their chances of selling their homes and resolving their tax debt. From working with a skilled agent to understanding the importance of pricing and marketing, these strategies can make a significant difference in the outcome of a property sale. With careful planning and expert guidance, it is possible to turn a difficult situation into a positive outcome for both the property owner and the buyer.

Chapter Eight

Tax Nightmares: Real-Life Stories of Property Tax Liens and Their Consequences

In this chapter, we'll delve into real-life examples of tax lien nightmares that can cause significant financial and personal distress for property owners. The stories of David, Linda, and Mike illustrate the severe consequences of ignoring tax obligations, falling behind on property tax payments, and accumulating tax debt. These examples demonstrate that tax liens can result in the seizure of assets, damage to credit scores, and the loss of potential profits. To prevent such situations, staying on top of tax payments and seeking professional help if struggling to make payments is essential.

The minimum amount that can result in foreclosure due to property tax liens varies by state, highlighting the importance of understanding the laws in a specific jurisdiction. It is crucial for property owners to know the law in their area to take proactive steps to prevent tax liens and avoid the devastating consequences that can result. In this chapter, we will explore how to avoid falling behind on property tax payments, the steps property owners can take to prevent tax liens, and how to navigate the process of selling a property with a tax lien. We will also discuss the different types of tax lien releases, including the IRS certificate of release, the release of lien or discharge of property, subordination, and withdrawal.

Overcoming Delinquent Property Taxes

Navigating property tax liens and the potential consequences can be challenging, but having specialized expertise and knowledge is key to avoiding financial hardship. By taking proactive steps to prevent tax liens, staying up-to-date on tax payments, and seeking professional help when needed, property owners can avoid the devastating consequences that can result from tax liens.

When we think of foreclosures, we typically associate them with delinquent mortgage payments. However, property tax liens can also result in foreclosure, and the consequences can be just as severe. In this situation, the local government places a lien on the property for unpaid property taxes, which can accumulate over time with interest and penalties. If the owner does not pay the taxes, the property can be sold at a public auction, often with all belongings inside. This provides an opportunity for investors nationwide to purchase properties at a low cost and resell them for a profit. Property tax lien foreclosures can be a complicated and costly process for property owners, making it crucial to stay on top of tax payments to avoid the risk of foreclosure.

In this chapter, you can take a look at some real-life examples of tax lien nightmares that can cause significant financial and personal distress:

Example 1: The Small Business Owner

David was the owner of a small construction company.

David's story is one of financial hardship and the devastating impact of tax liens. As the owner of a small construction company, David had always found it difficult to make ends meet. Despite his best efforts, he fell behind on his tax payments, and the IRS filed a tax lien against his property. This legal claim against his assets meant that David was unable to sell or refinance his property until the tax debt was paid in full.

As time passed, the amount of the tax debt continued to grow, and David found himself in a difficult situation. He was unable to pay the debt, and the IRS began to take steps to collect the money owed. Eventually, David was left with no choice but to sell his home to pay off the debt. This was a devastating blow for David, as he had invested so much time and energy into building his business and had hoped to pass it on to his children one day.

Unfortunately, the sale of his home was not enough to cover the full amount of the tax debt, and David was forced to use the proceeds to pay off what he could. This meant that he lost not only his home but also his business, as he no longer had the funds to keep it afloat. It was a crushing blow for David, who had worked so hard to build a life for himself and his family.

Example 2: The Real Estate Investor

Linda's story is a cautionary tale for real estate investors who are not diligent in paying their taxes. As a successful real estate investor, Linda had purchased several rental properties over the years. However, she had neglected to pay her taxes, and the IRS filed a tax lien against one of her properties.

Linda was shocked to learn that she could not sell the property without first paying off the tax debt. This was a major problem for her, as she had been planning to sell the property and use the proceeds to purchase a new investment. She was stuck with the property and accumulated debt without the ability to sell.

To resolve the situation, Linda had to use her savings to pay off the tax debt. This was a significant blow to her finances, as she had been counting on the profits from the sale to fund her next investment. Additionally, she lost out on the potential profit that could have been made from the sale of the property, as the longer she held onto it, the more her expenses continued to accumulate.

Example 3: The Self-Employed Professional

Mike's story is an example of the dangers of ignoring tax obligations and the severe consequences that can result. As a self-employed consultant, Mike had been struggling to make ends meet, and he had fallen behind on his tax payments. He had ignored the notices from the IRS, and as a result, the agency filed a tax lien against his property.

Mike was devastated by the news, as he realized that he could not sell his home and move to a more affordable place. The tax lien had made it impossible for him to access the equity in his home, which he had hoped to use to pay off his debts and start fresh. The tax debt had continued to accrue, and the longer he ignored it, the worse his situation became.

To resolve the issue, Mike had to work out a payment plan with the IRS, which took years to pay off. This meant he was stuck with a large debt for an extended period, making it difficult for him to save or invest for his future. Additionally, his credit score suffered as a result of the tax lien, which made it harder for him to access credit or obtain loans.

These three real-life examples of tax lien nightmares illustrate the devastating impact that tax debts can have on individuals and their businesses. David, Linda, and Mike all found themselves in difficult situations due to tax liens, which can lead to the seizure of assets, damage to credit scores, and the loss of potential profits. These stories are a warning to taxpayers to stay on top of their tax obligations and seek professional help if they are struggling to make payments. Ignoring tax obligations can lead to severe consequences, and it is essential to take steps to prevent tax liens and resolve tax debt promptly to avoid financial hardship.

In the world of tax liens, the minimum amount that can result in foreclosure due to a property tax lien varies by state. Property owners must know the law in their specific jurisdiction, as the consequences of falling behind on property taxes can be severe. For instance, in California, property owners may face foreclosure if they fail to pay property taxes for five years or more. In Texas, property owners can face foreclosure after six months of delinquency on property taxes. In New York, property owners can face foreclosure after three years of unpaid taxes. In Florida, property owners can face foreclosure after two years of unpaid property taxes, while in Illinois, property owners can face foreclosure after two years of unpaid taxes.

To avoid the risk of foreclosure due to a property tax lien, property owners must stay up-to-date on their tax payments and understand the laws in their specific jurisdiction. Knowing the law can help property owners take proactive steps to prevent tax liens and avoid the devastating consequences that can result.

In conclusion, dealing with property tax liens and the possibility of foreclosure can be a daunting and overwhelming process for property owners. However, staying on top of tax payments and understanding the options available for resolving tax debt and avoiding the consequences of tax liens is essential. Seeking professional help from a real estate agent or tax professional can be critical in navigating the complexities of the system and making informed decisions. This chapter has provided real-life examples of the impact of property tax liens on small business owners, real estate investors, and self-employed professionals, highlighting the importance of taking proactive steps to prevent tax liens and resolve tax debt promptly. By staying informed about the laws and regulations in their specific jurisdiction, property owners can take the necessary steps to protect their assets and avoid financial hardship. Remember, ignoring tax obligations can lead to severe consequences, and it is essential to take action promptly to prevent tax liens and resolve tax debt before it leads to foreclosure.

Chapter Nine

Programs for Delinquent Property Owners: Exploring Home Affordable and Disaster Assistance Options

For homeowners who are struggling to make their mortgage payments and are facing delinquency or foreclosure, there are various programs available to provide assistance. These programs offer different solutions to help homeowners stay in their homes, modify their loans, or refinance their mortgages. In this chapter, we will explore some of the most popular programs available for delinquent property owners. We will discuss the benefits and drawbacks of each program and provide guidance on how to determine which one is the right fit for your unique situation. With the help of these programs, homeowners facing delinquency or foreclosure can find solutions to alleviate their financial burden and keep their homes.

Homeowners need to stay on top of their property tax payments to avoid the risk of a tax lien. If a lien is placed on their property, they should take immediate action to pay it off and prevent further financial and legal consequences. The consequences of a tax lien can be devastating, impacting both the homeowner's finances and their ability to sell or transfer ownership of their property.

Understanding the process of tax liens and taking proactive measures to prevent them is crucial for homeowners to protect their investments and their financial futures.

Owning a home is the cornerstone of the American dream, but it can quickly become a nightmare for some homeowners when they fall behind on their property taxes. The result can be a tax lien on the property, which can have severe financial and legal consequences. Fortunately, programs are available to help distressed homeowners settle their tax liens before the situation worsens.

One organization that offers assistance to distressed homeowners is the National Tax Lien Association (NTLA). The NTLA believes in the importance of home ownership and is committed to helping homeowners who are struggling to keep their homes. The organization offers a variety of local and national assistance programs to help homeowners settle their tax debts and avoid the negative implications of a tax lien.

One such program offered by the NTLA is tax lien financing. This program allows homeowners to borrow money to pay off their tax liens, with the lien serving as collateral for the loan. The interest rates for tax lien financing can be lower than traditional lending options, making it a more affordable solution for distressed homeowners.

Another program offered by the NTLA is tax lien

foreclosure prevention. This program assists homeowners at risk of losing their homes due to a tax lien. The NTLA works with local governments and other organizations to provide homeowners with options to settle their debts and avoid foreclosure.

Distressed homeowners need to seek out professional advice and guidance when dealing with tax liens. The NTLA and other organizations can provide the necessary support to help homeowners navigate the complex process of settling tax debts and avoiding the negative financial consequences of a tax lien. By taking proactive steps to address tax liens, distressed homeowners can protect their investments in their homes and avoid the devastating effects of foreclosure.

The Home Affordable Foreclosure Alternatives Program

The Home Affordable Foreclosure Alternatives Program (HAFA) is a program that was created as part of the Making Home Affordable (MHA) initiative, which was launched in response to the housing crisis that hit the United States in 2008. HAFA was designed to help homeowners struggling to keep up with their mortgage payments and who could not obtain a loan modification under the Home Affordable Modification Program (HAMP).

The goal of HAFA was to provide viable alternatives to foreclosure, such as a short sale or a deed-in-lieu of foreclosure, to eligible homeowners. By providing these alternatives, the program aimed to help homeowners avoid foreclosure and the negative consequences that come with it, such as damage to credit scores, the loss of their home, and additional fees and expenses.

HAFA was available to homeowners who met certain qualifications. To be eligible, homeowners had to have a mortgage owned or guaranteed by Fannie Mae or Freddie Mac, or they had to have a mortgage held by a participating servicer. Homeowners also had to have a financial hardship that made it difficult for them to keep up with their mortgage payments, and they had to be either delinquent on their mortgage payments or in danger of default.

Under HAFA, eligible homeowners who chose to participate could receive financial assistance to help with relocation costs and other expenses associated with the sale of their homes. They could also receive guidance and support from a housing counselor to help them navigate the process and make informed decisions about their options.

There were limits to the amount of financial assistance homeowners could receive under HAFA. For example, homeowners who participated in a short sale under the program could receive up to $10,000 in relocation assistance, while homeowners who participated in a deed-in-lieu of foreclosure could receive up to $3,000 in relocation assistance. One of the key benefits of HAFA was that it provided a streamlined and standardized process for homeowners to apply for and receive assistance. This helped to make the program more accessible and easier to navigate for homeowners who were already dealing with the stress and uncertainty of financial hardship and the prospect of losing their homes.

Since its launch, HAFA has helped thousands of homeowners avoid foreclosure and find a more sustainable solution to their financial difficulties. Although the program faced challenges, it remains one of the most successful initiatives to come out of the MHA program, and it has had a significant impact on the housing market by stabilizing home prices and reducing the number of foreclosures.

FHA Refinance Program for Homeowners with Negative Equity

For homeowners who are struggling with negative equity or owing more on their mortgage than the value of their property, the Federal Housing Administration (FHA) offers a valuable refinancing program. The program is designed to help eligible borrowers refinance their mortgage and potentially reduce their monthly payments, even if they are underwater on their loan.

To be eligible for the FHA Refinance for Borrowers with Negative Equity program, homeowners must meet certain criteria. They must be current on their mortgage payments, have a minimum credit score of 620, and have a debt-to-income ratio of no more than 50%. They must also have a loan-to-value (LTV) ratio of no more than 125%, which means that they can owe up to 125% of the current value of their home.

One of the key benefits of the FHA Refinance for Borrowers with Negative Equity program is that it allows eligible homeowners to refinance their mortgage into a new FHA-insured loan with a lower interest rate and more favorable terms. This can help to reduce monthly mortgage payments, lower the overall cost of the mortgage, and make it easier for homeowners to manage their financial obligations.

In addition, the program also offers certain incentives to encourage eligible homeowners to participate. For example, homeowners who refinance through the program may be eligible for a reduction in their upfront mortgage insurance premium (MIP), which can help lower the overall mortgage cost.

Overall, the FHA Refinance for Borrowers with Negative Equity program is an important initiative providing valuable support to homeowners struggling with negative equity. By offering a path to refinancing that can help reduce monthly mortgage payments and improve overall affordability, the program helps promote financial stability and ensure that homeowners can manage their financial obligations. Whether you are underwater on your mortgage or simply looking for a more affordable way to manage your monthly payments, the FHA Refinance for Borrowers with a Negative Equity program may be an option to consider.

Home Affordable Unemployment Program

For many homeowners, the loss of a job can be a major financial setback that makes it difficult to keep up with mortgage payments and avoid foreclosure. To address this issue, the Home Affordable Unemployment Program (UP) was established as part of the broader Making Home Affordable (MHA) program.

The Home Affordable Unemployment Program aims to provide temporary financial assistance to eligible homeowners experiencing unemployment or other financial hardships. The program is designed to provide a safety net that can help prevent foreclosure and provide much-needed relief to homeowners struggling to manage their financial obligations.

To be eligible for the Home Affordable Unemployment Program, homeowners must meet certain criteria. They must be unemployed and actively seeking employment or have experienced a significant reduction in income due to a change in job or other circumstances. They must also have a mortgage that is owned or guaranteed by Fannie Mae or Freddie Mac, be delinquent or at risk of delinquency, and have a debt-to-income ratio of no more than 55%.

Homeowners who meet these requirements may be eligible for temporary financial assistance through the program. This assistance may take the form of a forbearance, which allows eligible homeowners to temporarily reduce or suspend their mortgage payments for up to 12 months. During this time, homeowners may also be eligible for other forms of support, such as job training and placement services, that can help them to get back on their feet and regain their financial stability.

The Home Affordable Unemployment Program is an important initiative providing much-needed support to homeowners struggling with financial hardship and unemployment. By providing temporary financial assistance and other forms of support, the program helps to prevent foreclosure and promote financial stability. Whether you are currently unemployed or simply looking for a way to manage your financial obligations, the Home Affordable Unemployment Program may be an option to consider.

FEMA Housing Portal

When natural disasters strike, they can have devastating effects on communities and individuals. In addition to the emotional toll, these events can also create significant challenges for those who are displaced from their homes and left without a place to stay. To help address this issue, the Federal Emergency Management Agency (FEMA) has created the FEMA Housing Portal.

The FEMA Housing Portal is a valuable resource that provides individuals and families with access to temporary housing options in the aftermath of a natural disaster. Through the portal, individuals can search for available housing options, including hotels, apartments, and other forms of temporary housing.

To use the FEMA Housing Portal, individuals simply need to create an account and provide information about their housing needs and preferences. They can then search for available housing options and make reservations directly through the portal. In addition, the portal also provides access to other forms of support, such as financial assistance and case management services, that can help individuals and families to get back on their feet and regain their stability.

One of the key benefits of the FEMA Housing Portal is that it provides individuals with a central location to access a range of different housing options and support services. This can help to simplify the process of finding temporary housing and provide individuals with the resources they need to navigate the aftermath of a natural disaster. In addition, the portal also provides a valuable platform for connecting with others who may be facing similar challenges and sharing information about available resources and support services.

Overall, the FEMA Housing Portal is an important resource

that provides critical support to displaced individuals and families in the aftermath of a natural disaster. Whether you are searching for temporary housing or simply looking for support and guidance during a difficult time, the portal can be a valuable tool to help you navigate disaster recovery challenges.

Home and Property Disaster Loans

Natural disasters can strike at any time and significantly impact communities and individuals. In addition to the emotional toll, these events can also cause significant damage to homes and properties, leaving individuals with the daunting task of rebuilding and recovering.

To help address this issue, the Small Business Administration (SBA) offers Home and Property Disaster Loans. These loans provide critical financial assistance to individuals and businesses that have been affected by natural disasters and are in need of funding to repair or replace damaged property.

Home and Property Disaster Loans are available to individuals who own their own homes and to renters and businesses. The loans can be used to repair or replace damaged or destroyed real estate, personal property, and other items affected by a natural disaster. In addition, the loans can also be used to cover costs related to temporary housing and other essential expenses that may arise in the aftermath of a disaster.

To be eligible for a Home and Property Disaster Loan, individuals must have suffered damage or loss as a result of a declared disaster. They must also have a credit score that meets the SBA's minimum requirements and be able to demonstrate the ability to repay the loan. The loan amount that individuals may be eligible for will depend on a variety of factors, including the extent of the damage and the individual's financial situation.

One of the key benefits of Home and Property Disaster Loans is that they provide individuals with the financial resources they need to recover and rebuild after a natural disaster. This can help to alleviate some of the stress and uncertainty that can arise in the aftermath of a disaster and provide individuals with the support they need to move forward and regain their stability.

Overall, Home and Property Disaster Loans are an important resource for individuals and businesses that have been affected by natural disasters. Whether you are a homeowner, renter, or business owner, these loans can provide critical financial assistance that can help you to recover and rebuild after a difficult and challenging time.

Individuals and Household Program - Housing Assistance (IHP)

When disaster strikes, it can have a major effect on individuals and families. Not only can it cause emotional distress and upheaval, but it can also leave individuals without a place to call home. To help address this issue, the Federal Emergency Management Agency (FEMA) offers the Individuals and Household Program - Housing Assistance (IHP).

IHP provides critical financial assistance to individuals and households that have been affected by a disaster and are in need of housing support. The program offers two types of housing assistance: temporary housing and home repair.

Temporary housing assistance is designed to provide individuals and households with a safe and secure place to stay while they work to recover from a disaster. This can include rental assistance for a temporary residence, as well as assistance with the cost of hotel or motel rooms.

Home repair assistance is designed to help individuals and households to repair or replace damaged or destroyed homes. This can include assistance with the cost of repairs, as well as help with the cost of replacing essential household items that have been lost or damaged in the disaster.

To be eligible for IHP housing assistance, individuals and households must be located in a declared disaster area and have suffered damage or loss as a result of the disaster. They must also be able to demonstrate that they have no other housing options available and have an immediate housing need.

One of the key benefits of IHP housing assistance is that it provides critical support to individuals and households who have been affected by a disaster. This can help to alleviate some of the stress and uncertainty that can arise in the aftermath of a disaster and provide individuals and households with the support they need to move forward and rebuild.

Overall, the Individuals and Household Program - Housing Assistance (IHP) is an important resource for individuals and households that have been affected by a disaster. Whether you are in need of temporary housing or home repair assistance, the program can provide critical financial support that can help you to recover and rebuild after a difficult and challenging time.

203(h) Mortgage Insurance for Disaster Victims

The 203(h) Mortgage Insurance for Disaster Victims program is designed to provide mortgage insurance to individuals and families who have lost their homes or experienced significant damage as a result of a disaster. This program allows borrowers to obtain a new mortgage or rebuild their home with an existing mortgage, even if they have experienced financial hardship due to the disaster.

One of the key benefits of the 203(h) Mortgage Insurance for Disaster Victims program is that it provides a lifeline for homeowners who have been affected by a disaster. This program allows borrowers to purchase or refinance a home with a low down payment and at a competitive interest rate, even if they have limited financial resources. The program also allows borrowers to finance the cost of repairs or renovations into their mortgage, making it easier to afford these expenses.

To be eligible for the 203(h) Mortgage Insurance for Disaster Victims program, borrowers must live in a presidentially declared disaster area and have suffered damage or loss to their homes as a result of the disaster. They must also be able to demonstrate that they had a good credit history prior to the disaster and that they are willing and able to repay the loan.

Overall, the 203(h) Mortgage Insurance for Disaster Victims program is an important resource for homeowners who have been affected by a disaster. This program can provide critical financial assistance to help borrowers rebuild their homes and their lives in the aftermath of a disaster. By providing low down payments and competitive interest rates, this program can help to make homeownership a reality for those who may not have been able to afford it otherwise.

FHA Loan Modification

FHA loans are a popular financing option for many homeowners due to their flexible credit requirements and low down payment options. However, sometimes unexpected financial hardships can occur, making it difficult for homeowners to make their mortgage payments. In these situations, an FHA loan modification may be a viable solution.

An FHA loan modification is a type of mortgage refinancing that allows homeowners to adjust their monthly mortgage payments to better fit their current financial situation. This modification is available to borrowers who are having difficulty making their current mortgage payments due to a temporary financial hardship such as job loss, medical emergency, or a significant increase in expenses.

The FHA loan modification program is designed to help eligible borrowers avoid foreclosure by adjusting their mortgage payments to a more manageable level. The modification may involve a reduction in interest rate, an extension of the loan term, or a combination of both.

To qualify for an FHA loan modification, borrowers must demonstrate that they are experiencing a significant financial hardship that is affecting their ability to make their mortgage payments. Additionally, they must have a history of making their mortgage payments on time prior to the financial hardship.

The FHA loan modification process can be complex and requires the submission of a variety of financial documents to verify income, expenses, and other financial obligations. It is recommended that borrowers work with a HUD-approved housing counselor or a loan modification specialist to help navigate the process.

While an FHA loan modification can be a valuable tool for homeowners facing financial hardship, it is important to remember that it is not a permanent solution. The modification may provide temporary relief, but it is essential for borrowers to create a long-term financial plan to ensure their continued success in making mortgage payments and maintaining their homes.

VA Purchase & Cash-Out Refinance Home Loans

As a veteran or a service member, you might have availed yourself of a VA loan to purchase a home. However, unforeseen circumstances such as financial difficulties or loss of income can make it challenging to keep up with the mortgage payments. In such cases, the VA loan modification program can help you restructure your loan to make it more affordable and prevent foreclosure.

The VA loan modification program is designed to help veterans and service members who are struggling to make their mortgage payments. Through this program, you can work with your lender to modify the terms of your existing VA loan to make it more affordable.

The loan modification process involves changing the loan agreement terms to reduce the monthly payment amount or extend the loan term. In some cases, the lender may also reduce the interest rate or forgive part of the principal balance to make the loan more affordable.

To qualify for a VA loan modification, you must demonstrate that you are facing a financial hardship that is making it difficult to make your mortgage payments. This may include a significant reduction in income, a job loss, or a medical emergency that has caused unexpected expenses.

The VA loan modification program has several benefits for borrowers. For one, it can help you avoid foreclosure and stay in your home. Additionally, it can provide you with more affordable monthly payments, making it easier to manage your finances and stay on track.

You can contact your lender or speak with a VA loan specialist to learn more about the VA loan modification program. They can provide you with more information about the program's eligibility requirements and help you navigate the application process.

Fannie Mae Flex Modification

Fannie Mae Flex Modification is a foreclosure prevention program that offers eligible borrowers a more affordable mortgage payment. The program is designed to help homeowners avoid foreclosure and stay in their homes.

Fannie Mae Flex Modification was introduced in 2017 to replace the Home Affordable Modification Program (HAMP), which was created in 2009 as a response to the housing crisis. The program is available for mortgages that are owned or guaranteed by Fannie Mae.

The Flex Modification program is designed to help borrowers who are at least 60 days' delinquent on their mortgage payments or facing imminent default. The goal is to reduce the borrower's monthly mortgage payment by at least 20 percent by modifying the terms of the loan.

The program offers a number of modification options, including a reduction in the interest rate, extending the loan term, and deferring a portion of the principal balance. The program may also offer a forbearance, which temporarily suspends or reduces mortgage payments for a specific period of time.

To be eligible for Fannie Mae Flex Modification, borrowers must meet certain requirements. Borrowers must have a Fannie Mae-owned or guaranteed mortgage, be at least 60 days delinquent on their mortgage payments or face imminent default, and have a debt-to-income ratio of 80 percent or higher. Borrowers may also be required to provide documentation to verify their income and hardship.

It is important to note that the guidelines for the Fannie Mae

Flex Modification program are subject to change. Borrowers should always check with their mortgage servicer or a housing counselor for the latest information on eligibility and requirements.

USDA Special Loan Servicing

For rural Americans facing financial difficulties, the United States Department of Agriculture (USDA) offers Special Loan Servicing to help alleviate their burden. These services are designed for borrowers who are experiencing hardships and struggling to meet their mortgage obligations. The program is intended to prevent foreclosure and ensure homeownership remains a possibility for those who may have fallen on hard times.

USDA Special Loan Servicing is available for those who hold a USDA Rural Development (RD) loan for their home. In cases where the borrower is unable to make their mortgage payments on time, Special Loan Servicing is offered to provide relief and assistance.

One of the key benefits of Special Loan Servicing is that it provides options for restructuring a borrower's loan. This may include a reduction in the interest rate, or an extension of the loan repayment term, to help make payments more manageable. For borrowers who have missed payments, a repayment plan may also be established to help get them back on track.

Another advantage of this program is that it offers loan

forbearance. Forbearance is a temporary period during which a borrower is not required to make payments on their mortgage. This is typically granted to borrowers who are experiencing significant financial hardship, such as a job loss or illness.

USDA Special Loan Servicing is available to rural Americans who are facing a variety of financial challenges, including natural disasters and other emergencies. This program can help provide assistance to those who need it most and ensure that they can continue to enjoy the benefits of homeownership.

It's important to note that not all borrowers will qualify for Special Loan Servicing. Borrowers must demonstrate that they have experienced a hardship that has impacted their ability to make mortgage payments. Furthermore, they must demonstrate a willingness and ability to repay their loan.

In conclusion, buying a home is one of the most significant investments anyone can make in their lifetime. It is an opportunity to plant roots, build equity, and make memories. However, with homeownership also comes the possibility of financial hardship. Life can take unexpected turns, leaving homeowners struggling to keep up with mortgage payments, facing foreclosure, or experiencing homelessness.

Fortunately, housing counseling agencies are available throughout the country to provide guidance and advice to homeowners in need. These agencies offer free foreclosure prevention counseling, homeless counseling, and low-cost counseling for other housing-related issues. They are staffed by trained professionals who understand the complexities of the housing market and can offer customized solutions to fit each homeowner's unique situation.

There are many benefits to using a housing counselor when faced with financial hardship. First and foremost, a counselor can help homeowners understand their rights and options. They can explain the various government programs available to homeowners, such as loan modifications, refinancing, or forbearance, and help homeowners determine which options may be best for their specific circumstances.

Additionally, a housing counselor can provide homeowners with the knowledge and skills necessary to navigate the often-complicated process of dealing with lenders and mortgage servicers. They can help homeowners communicate with their lenders effectively, negotiate loan terms, and even attend mediation sessions with the lender on behalf of the homeowner.

Housing counselors can also help homeowners develop a budget and create a plan to get back on track financially. They can review a homeowner's income and expenses, identify areas where money can be saved, and create a plan to pay off debts or catch up on mortgage payments.

Finally, housing counselors can provide emotional support to homeowners who may be struggling with the stress and anxiety that comes with financial hardship. They can be a source of encouragement and offer resources to help homeowners cope with the challenges they are facing.

In conclusion, several programs are available for those struggling with delinquent property payments. From the Home Affordable Modification Program to the FHA Refinance for Borrowers with Negative Equity and the Home Affordable Unemployment Program, there are options to help individuals and families avoid foreclosure and keep their homes. Additionally, in the event of a disaster, programs such as the FEMA Housing Portal and Home and Property Disaster Loans can provide assistance to homeowners. It's important to explore all available options and seek professional help when dealing with delinquent property payments to avoid the risk of foreclosure and protect your home.

Chapter Ten

Navigating Foreclosure: Strategies for Resolving Property Tax Debt and Protecting Your Home

Foreclosure can be a daunting and stressful process for any homeowner, but it becomes especially complex when property taxes are involved. Whether it's due to financial hardship, delinquency, or other unforeseen circumstances, it's crucial for property owners to understand the ins and outs of foreclosure and how it can affect their property, finances, and future prospects.

In this chapter, we will delve into the different types of foreclosure, including non-judicial and judicial foreclosure, and explore the implications of each. We will also discuss the eviction process, the right of redemption, and excess money that can arise from the foreclosure sale. Additionally, we will look into alternatives to foreclosure, such as equitable pre-foreclosure and statutory right of redemption, and the importance of reading the fine print.

Furthermore, we will touch on the difficulty of finding a new place to call home and the potential implications on buying a home in the future. We will also provide information on how to avoid foreclosure through lenders and the role of foreclosure avoidance counselors.

By understanding the foreclosure process and the options available to them, property owners can take steps to protect their assets and their financial future. Whether you are currently facing foreclosure or seeking to prevent it, this chapter will provide valuable insights and resources to help navigate the complex world of property taxes and foreclosure.

When it comes to tax liens, homeowners may find themselves facing the possibility of foreclosure. There are two types of foreclosures: judicial and non-judicial.

A judicial foreclosure involves going through a court, where the lender will file a lawsuit against the homeowner to obtain a court order to foreclose on the property. This process can take some time and involve multiple court hearings.

In contrast, a non-judicial foreclosure doesn't involve the court system. Instead, the lender will follow the foreclosure procedures written into the mortgage contract. This type of foreclosure is typically faster and more streamlined than a judicial foreclosure.

However, the type of foreclosure also affects the procedures and defenses that can be raised. In a judicial foreclosure, the homeowner may have more opportunities to challenge the foreclosure and present defenses in court. In a non-judicial foreclosure, the homeowner may have fewer opportunities to do so.

Furthermore, the type of foreclosure can also affect whether the foreclosed-on homeowner will be liable for a deficiency after the foreclosure sale. A deficiency occurs when the foreclosure sale doesn't generate enough money to pay off the full amount owed on the mortgage. In a judicial foreclosure, the lender may be able to obtain a deficiency judgment against the homeowner for the remaining amount owed. In a non-judicial foreclosure, the lender may not be able to obtain a deficiency judgment.

Facing a tax lien foreclosure can be a stressful and overwhelming experience. That's why it's important for homeowners to understand the different types of foreclosures and the implications of each. Seeking the guidance of a qualified attorney or housing counselor can help homeowners navigate the process and potentially avoid foreclosure altogether.

Understanding Non-Judicial Foreclosure

Non-judicial foreclosure is a process that allows lenders to foreclose on a property without going through a court proceeding. It is also known as "power of sale" foreclosure because it is executed through the power of sale clause in the mortgage or deed of trust.

In non-judicial foreclosure, the lender is not required to go to court to initiate foreclosure proceedings. Instead, they follow the foreclosure procedures outlined in the mortgage or deed of trust, which typically involves giving notice to the borrower, advertising the foreclosure sale, and conducting a public auction of the property.

Non-judicial foreclosure is only available in certain states, and the rules and procedures vary by state. The following are some of the states that have non-judicial foreclosure procedures:

Alaska, Arizona, California, Colorado, Hawaii, Idaho, Montana, Nevada, New Mexico, North Carolina, Oregon, Texas, Utah, Washington, and Wyoming.

In some states, like California and Nevada, non-judicial foreclosure is the primary foreclosure method. In others, it is only available under certain circumstances or as an alternative to judicial foreclosure.

It's important to note that while non-judicial foreclosure can be a faster and less expensive process for lenders, it can also be more difficult for homeowners to challenge. Homeowners facing non-judicial foreclosure should consider seeking the advice of a qualified attorney to determine their legal options and defenses.

Navigating Judicial Foreclosure for Property Tax Debt

In a judicial foreclosure, the foreclosure process goes through the court system. This means that the lender must file a lawsuit against the borrower in order to foreclose on the property. The court then determines whether the borrower is in default and grants a foreclosure judgment if they are.

One advantage of judicial foreclosure is that it allows the borrower to raise defenses in court. These defenses might include arguments that the lender did not follow proper foreclosure procedures, that the borrower was not in default, or that the lender engaged in unfair lending practices.

However, the judicial foreclosure process can be time-consuming and expensive for both the lender and the borrower. The lender may also be required to pay certain court costs and attorney fees.

Judicial foreclosure is used in some states, while other states allow for non-judicial foreclosure. States that use judicial foreclosure include Florida, New York, Illinois, and New Jersey, among others.

Surplus Funds from Property Foreclosure

As a homeowner facing foreclosure, it is important to understand what happens to any remaining funds after the property has been foreclosed on. Once the lender has recouped the amount owed on the mortgage, they cannot keep the full sale price of the home.

The lender is entitled to keep all fees associated with the foreclosure process, such as legal fees and costs for the sale of the property. Any remaining funds are then used to pay off any outstanding liens on the property, such as a second mortgage or home equity line of credit. If there are no liens on the property, the remaining funds will be paid directly to the homeowner who lost the property to the foreclosure proceedings.

It's important to note that if there are existing liens on the property, the funds from the sale will be used to pay off those liens before you receive any remaining amount. This means that if the remaining amount is not enough to pay off all liens, the person or persons who lost the property may still owe money even after the sale of your property.

As a homeowner facing foreclosure, it's important to stay informed and be aware of your rights throughout the process. Understanding what happens to any remaining funds after the sale of your property is just one of the many important things to keep in mind.

Understanding the Eviction Process for Foreclosed Properties

Eviction is a process by which a property owner takes legal action to remove a tenant or occupant from their property. It can be a complicated process that requires both the homeowner and the occupants to understand their rights and responsibilities.

When a property is sold at foreclosure, the new owner may need to evict the occupants in order to take possession of the property. In some cases, the occupants may have rights that must be respected during this process. For example, if the occupants have a lease, the new owner must honor it until it expires.

The eviction process varies from state to state but generally involves several steps. First, the new owner must provide the occupants with a notice to vacate, which gives them a certain amount of time to leave the property. If the occupants do not leave, the new owner must file an eviction lawsuit in court.

The following are several examples of the eviction process in five different states:

1. California - In California, a landlord must first provide the tenant with a written notice to vacate. If the tenant does not vacate the property, the landlord can then file an unlawful detainer lawsuit. If the landlord prevails in the lawsuit, the tenant will be ordered to vacate the property. The eviction process can take anywhere from a few weeks to a few months.

2. Texas - In Texas, a landlord must also provide a tenant with a written notice to vacate before filing an eviction lawsuit. The notice must give the tenant at least three days to vacate the property. If the tenant does not vacate the property, the

landlord can file an eviction lawsuit. The eviction process can take around two to three weeks.

3. New York - In New York, the eviction process can vary depending on the specific circumstances of the case. However, generally, the landlord must provide the tenant with a notice to cure or quit, giving the tenant a certain amount of time to fix the issue or vacate the property. If the tenant does not comply, the landlord can file a petition in court. The eviction process can take several months.

4. Florida - In Florida, the eviction process also begins with a written notice to vacate. If the tenant does not vacate the property, the landlord can file an eviction lawsuit. If the landlord prevails, the tenant will be ordered to vacate the property within a set amount of time. The eviction process can take around three to four weeks.

5. Illinois - In Illinois, the eviction process also requires a written notice to vacate before the landlord can file an eviction lawsuit. The notice must give the tenant a certain amount of time to vacate the property. The landlord can file an eviction lawsuit if the tenant does not vacate. The eviction process can take around three to four weeks.

In some states, the eviction process can be relatively quick, while in others, it can be a lengthy and complicated process. It's important for both the new owner and the occupants to understand their rights and responsibilities during the eviction process.

During the eviction lawsuit, the court will determine whether the new owner has the legal right to evict the occupants. If the court rules in favor of the new owner, the occupants will be given a certain amount of time to leave the property. If they do not leave, the new owner may need to hire a sheriff or other law enforcement officer to physically remove the occupants from the property.

Occupants have the right to a fair and reasonable eviction process. They may be able to negotiate with the new owner or work out an agreement allowing them to stay in the property for a certain period. In some cases, occupants may be entitled to compensation or relocation assistance to help them find new housing.

The new owner also has certain rights during the eviction process. They have the right to take legal action to remove the occupants from the property if necessary. They may also be entitled to compensation for any damages or expenses incurred during the eviction process.

Overall, the eviction process can be a complicated and emotional experience for both the occupants and the new owner. It's important for all parties to understand their rights and responsibilities and to work together to ensure a fair and reasonable outcome.

Redemption Rights for Property Owners Facing Foreclosure

The right of redemption after an eviction is the right of the former homeowner to buy back their property within a certain timeframe after the foreclosure sale. The terms of this right vary by state and can significantly impact the former homeowner's ability to reclaim their property.

In some states, the right of redemption is limited to a certain period of time after the foreclosure sale. For example, in California, the redemption period is one year after the sale, and in Minnesota, it is six months. In other states, the right of redemption may not exist at all or may be limited in other ways. In Texas, for example, there is no right of redemption for foreclosed properties, while in Florida, the right of redemption only applies to properties sold at a tax deed sale.

In Alabama, the right of redemption lasts for one year after the sale, but the former homeowner must pay the full amount of the sale price, plus interest and other fees. In contrast, in Illinois, the right of redemption lasts for 180 days, and the former homeowner must pay the sale price plus interest at a rate set by the court.

In Tennessee, the right of redemption applies to properties sold at a tax sale and lasts for one year. However, the former homeowner must pay the sale price, interest and other fees, and any taxes owed on the property.

In summary, the right of redemption after an eviction varies widely by state and can have significant consequences for former homeowners seeking to reclaim their property. Homeowners need to understand their state's specific policies and timelines in order to make informed decisions about their options after a foreclosure sale.

Understanding Equitable Pre-Foreclosure in Property Tax Liens

As homeowners, we all want to avoid foreclosure and the stress and uncertainty that comes with it. One option available to homeowners facing financial hardship is equitable pre-foreclosure.

Equitable pre-foreclosure is a process by which homeowners can sell their property before foreclosure proceedings begin. It allows the homeowner to avoid the negative effects of foreclosure on their credit score while still being able to pay off the outstanding balance on their mortgage.

In an equitable pre-foreclosure, the homeowner will work with the lender to sell the property for an amount that is equal to or greater than the outstanding balance on the mortgage. The lender will agree to accept the sale proceeds in full satisfaction of the debt, thus avoiding foreclosure proceedings.

The key benefit of an equitable pre-foreclosure is that it

allows the homeowner to avoid foreclosure and the negative effects it can have on their credit score. It can also allow the homeowner to sell the property for a higher price than they would in a foreclosure auction, as they have more control over the sale.

Equitable pre-foreclosure is not available in all states, and the specifics of the process can vary from state to state. In some states, it is known as a short sale, while in others, it is referred to as a pre-foreclosure sale. It is important to consult with a qualified real estate attorney or housing counselor to fully understand the process and its implications.

Overall, an equitable pre-foreclosure can be a viable option for homeowners facing financial hardship and the threat of foreclosure. It allows them to take control of the situation and work with their lender to find a solution that benefits everyone involved.

Understanding the Statutory Right of Redemption

Imagine losing your property through foreclosure. It's a tough pill to swallow, but what if you had an opportunity to get it back? The statutory right of redemption offers homeowners a chance to recover their foreclosed properties after the foreclosure sale. It may seem too good to be true, but this right is granted to homeowners in some states.

The statutory right of redemption is a legal provision that grants homeowners the right to repurchase their foreclosed properties within a specified period. In some states, this period ranges from a few days to one year after the foreclosure sale, depending on the state laws. During this period, the homeowner has the right to reclaim the property by paying off the full amount owed to the foreclosing lender, plus any additional fees and costs incurred during the foreclosure process.

While the statutory right of redemption offers homeowners a second chance to keep their properties, it's important to note that it doesn't come without costs. The homeowner must pay the full amount owed on the mortgage, usually the foreclosure sale amount. Additionally, the homeowner must also pay any additional fees and costs incurred during the foreclosure process, such as attorney fees, court fees, and other related expenses.

Not all states offer a statutory right of redemption and those that do have varying timeframes and conditions. For example, in Mississippi, homeowners have one year to redeem their foreclosed properties but must pay the full amount owed plus ten percent interest. On the other hand, in Tennessee, homeowners have only ten days to redeem their foreclosed properties, but they only need to pay the purchase price plus interest and expenses incurred during the foreclosure process.

The statutory right of redemption is a valuable option for homeowners who wish to reclaim their foreclosed properties. It offers them a chance to rectify the default and keep their homes. However, the decision to redeem a foreclosed property should not be taken lightly. It's important to weigh the costs and benefits carefully, including the amount of the redemption price and any additional fees and costs. Homeowners should also seek legal advice to ensure that they fully understand the redemption process and their rights under state laws.

In conclusion, the statutory right of redemption is a lifeline for homeowners who have lost their homes through foreclosure. While the timeframes and conditions vary across states, the right offers homeowners a second chance to keep their homes by repurchasing them. However, the process can be complicated and costly, so homeowners should weigh their options and seek legal advice before deciding to redeem their foreclosed properties.

Time-Sensitive Solutions to Save Your Home from Foreclosure

Foreclosure can be a daunting and overwhelming process for any homeowner. However, it is important to remember that you may have some options to save your home, particularly if you are in a right-of-redemption jurisdiction with a long redemption period. This means you may have anywhere from a few months to a year or more to save your home, depending on your state's laws.

It is crucial that you act quickly and according to a plan if you want to save your home from foreclosure. This means that you should take steps to repay any outstanding property taxes and homeowner's insurance, if applicable. If you don't, you may find yourself facing additional tax liens or even a liability suit or casualty loss, which will only compound your problems.

One of the first things you should do if you are facing foreclosure is to get in touch with your lender. They may be willing to work with you to find a solution that allows you to keep your home. This may include a loan modification, which can help you to lower your monthly payments and make them more affordable. Your lender may also be willing to negotiate a repayment plan that allows you to catch up on missed payments over time.

If you are in a non-judicial foreclosure state, you will typically have a shorter amount of time to get your affairs in order. In some cases, the foreclosure process may take as little as a few months. In a judicial foreclosure state, however, the process can take much longer, often up to a year or more. This can give you more time to get your finances in order and take steps to save your home.

In any case, it is important that you act quickly and decisively if you want to save your home from foreclosure. This means that you should take steps to get your finances in order, get in touch with your lender, and work with them to find a solution that works for you. With the right approach, you can save your home and protect your investment for the future.

Understanding the Fine Print: Essential Details for Dealing with Property Tax Liens

Facing foreclosure can be a daunting experience, and it's important to take proactive steps to save your home. Once the process has begun, it's critical to review all the correspondence from your lender and understand your rights and options. Take the time to review your mortgage documents as well to ensure you have a clear understanding of the terms and conditions of your loan.

One crucial factor to consider is the timeline for the foreclosure process. Depending on your state and the specific circumstances of your case, the timeline can vary greatly. It's important to find out the timeline in your state so that you can act quickly and efficiently to save your home.

Another important consideration is whether any deficiency judgments are applicable in your case. These judgments can hold you personally responsible for the difference between your outstanding loan balance and what your home ultimately sells for. It's important to understand if deficiency judgments are a factor in your case and take appropriate steps to avoid them.

Finally, it's important to determine if a redemption right is available in your state. This grace period can allow you to reverse your foreclosure and keep your home. If the right of redemption is available to you, it's critical to act quickly and follow the necessary steps to take advantage of this opportunity.

In conclusion, taking proactive steps to save your home is critical if you are facing foreclosure. By reviewing all correspondence and understanding your rights and options, you can take the necessary steps to save your home and avoid the devastating consequences of losing it.

Getting Help from Foreclosure Avoidance Counselors

If you are facing the possibility of foreclosure, it's important to seek help from a HUD-approved housing counselor as soon as possible. These counselors are trained to help you understand your options and work with you to develop a plan to avoid foreclosure.

To find a HUD-approved housing counselor, you can visit the HUD website or call their toll-free hotline. The website has a searchable database of counselors by state and zip code, making it easy to find someone in your area. The hotline is staffed by trained counselors who can provide information and help you connect with a local counselor.

When working with a HUD-approved housing counselor, being open and honest about your situation is important. They will need to understand your income, expenses, and debts in order to help you create a plan that works for you. They may be able to negotiate with your lender on your behalf or help you explore options like loan modification or refinancing.

Remember, the earlier you seek help, the more options you will have. Don't wait until you're in the middle of foreclosure proceedings to reach out for help. A HUD-approved housing counselor can be a valuable resource to help you avoid foreclosure and keep your home.

Alternatives to Foreclosure Through Lenders: Exploring Your Options

When faced with the possibility of foreclosure, knowing that you have options is essential. Foreclosure doesn't have to be the end of the line for homeowners who are struggling to make their mortgage payments. One of the best alternatives to foreclosure is to work with your lender to find a solution.

Lenders have a vested interest in keeping you in your home and avoiding foreclosure. There are many programs available to help struggling homeowners, including loan modifications, repayment plans, and forbearance. These programs can reduce your monthly payments and help you get back on track.

If you're considering working with your lender, it's important to be proactive and take action as soon as possible. The longer you wait, the fewer options you will have. Being open and honest with your lender about your financial situation is also crucial. Lenders are more likely to work with borrowers who are transparent and willing to find a solution.

Another option is to work with a housing counselor approved by the Department of Housing and Urban Development (HUD). These counselors can provide free or low-cost assistance to homeowners who are facing foreclosure. They can help you understand your options, negotiate with your lender, and develop a plan to avoid foreclosure.

To find a HUD-approved housing counselor, you can visit the HUD website or call their toll-free number. A counselor will work with you to evaluate your financial situation and develop a plan that works for you.

In conclusion, there are many alternatives to foreclosure, and working with your lender is one of the best options. By being proactive and seeking assistance from a HUD-approved housing counselor, you can find a solution that works for you and keep your home. Remember, foreclosure doesn't have to be the end of the line, and there is always help available.

Consequences of Foreclosure

Foreclosure is a deeply painful and personal experience that can have significant and long-lasting effects on the individual who has lost their property. Losing a home is one of the most traumatic events that a person can go through, and it can be difficult to recover from the emotional toll that comes with it.

Foreclosure can lead to a sense of hopelessness and despair, as the person who has lost their property may feel like they have failed in some way. The stress and anxiety of the situation can also take a toll on one's mental and physical health, leading to depression, insomnia, and even physical ailments like heart disease or high blood pressure.

In addition to the emotional and physical toll, foreclosure can have a lasting impact on a person's financial future. A foreclosure can significantly impact your credit scores with Equifax, Experian, and TransUnion, the three major credit bureaus. A foreclosure will negatively impact your credit score and stay on your credit report for seven years. This will make it harder for you to obtain credit in the future, and you may be subject to higher interest rates.

When a foreclosure occurs, it is reported to the credit bureaus, and your credit score will drop immediately. The exact amount of the drop will depend on your current credit score, but typically it can be between 100 and 300 points. This significant drop in your credit score can make it harder to obtain credit in the future, and it may also impact your ability to rent a home, get a job, or obtain insurance.

The impact of a foreclosure on your credit score can be long-lasting. Even after the foreclosure is removed from your credit report after seven years, the damage has been done. It may still be harder for you to obtain credit, and you may have to pay higher interest rates. This is why it is important to try to avoid foreclosure if possible and work with your lender to find alternatives.

Moreover, the process of foreclosure can leave individuals feeling powerless and out of control as they are forced to navigate a complex and often overwhelming legal system. It is important to seek resources and support during this time, such as legal aid, counseling, or community organizations specializing in foreclosure prevention.

In the end, the impact of foreclosure on an individual cannot be overstated. It can have long-lasting emotional, physical, and financial effects that can take years to overcome. It is crucial to take steps to prevent foreclosure whenever possible and to seek out support and resources if you find yourself facing this difficult situation.

Challenges of Finding a New Home After Foreclosure

After losing a home to foreclosure, the reality of finding a new place to rent can be daunting. Landlords are wary of renting to someone with a foreclosure record, and the hurdles can seem insurmountable. Most landlords require a cash deposit, which can be a huge barrier to overcome. In some cases, landlords will demand a double deposit, meaning that you will need to come up with twice the amount of money upfront just to secure a rental property.

Furthermore, landlords will often look at your credit score and history as a way to assess your financial responsibility. Unfortunately, a foreclosure severely damages your credit score and will significantly limit your options. Most landlords will require a credit score of at least 620, but some may accept lower scores in the range of 580 to 600. However, even with a lower score, you will need to prove that you have a reliable and long-term job history. This means that losing your home can have long-lasting consequences, affecting not only your living situation but also your employment prospects.

Once you have found a place to rent, you will still need to face the difficult task of relocating your personal items. You will have at least a few days to remove your belongings from your foreclosed home, but this will generally not be enough time to find another place to live. Relocating your belongings can be costly and time-consuming, particularly if you have a lot of items to move. Hiring a moving company can be expensive, and finding affordable options may be difficult, particularly if you have limited financial resources.

The harsh reality of trying to find a place to rent after a

foreclosure can be overwhelming. It can seem as though everything is stacked against you, and the road ahead can be long and difficult. However, it's essential to remember that you are not alone. There are resources available to help you navigate this challenging time, and with determination and perseverance, you can find a new place to call home.

Purchasing a Home After Dealing with Property Tax Issues

Buying a home after a foreclosure can be a difficult decision, and many people wonder if it's even possible. The good news is that it is possible but may require a lot of work, patience, and financial planning. The bad news is that rebuilding your credit score and saving up for a down payment will take time and effort.

If you have a foreclosure, your credit score will take a hit, and it can be challenging to get a mortgage loan from a traditional lender. However, there are options available to help people who have gone through foreclosure to become homeowners again.

One option is to look into loans offered by the Federal Housing Administration (FHA), Fannie Mae, or the Department of Veterans Affairs (VA). FHA and VA loans have more lenient credit score requirements than traditional loans, and they may be able to offer you a better interest rate. Fannie Mae offers a program called the "Back to Work" program, which helps people who have gone through foreclosure to qualify for a loan.

Before applying for a loan, it's important to make sure that you're financially prepared. You'll need to save up for a down payment and ensure you can afford the monthly mortgage payments. It's also important to work on rebuilding your credit score.

The amount of time that must pass after a foreclosure before someone can qualify for a conventional loan is typically seven years. However, if there were extenuating circumstances such as job loss or medical issues, this may be reduced to three years. For an FHA loan, the waiting period is generally three years but can be reduced to one year with extenuating circumstances. VA loans have the shortest waiting period, with only a two-year waiting period required. It's important to note that these waiting periods can vary based on individual circumstances and lender requirements, so it's always best to consult with a lender to determine your specific eligibility.

If you're considering buying a home after foreclosure, it's important to take your time and do your research. You'll need to find a lender willing to work with you, and it's important to understand the requirements and guidelines for the loan programs you're considering.

In conclusion, understanding the implications of property tax liens and foreclosures is crucial for property owners to protect their assets and avoid financial hardship. There are various options available for dealing with property tax liens, including payment plans, loan options, and government programs. It is essential to stay informed of the options available and seek professional help if needed to avoid the severe consequences of tax liens and foreclosures.

In this chapter, we discuss the foreclosure process, including non-judicial and judicial foreclosure, the eviction process, and the right of redemption. It is crucial to understand the foreclosure process and the potential consequences, such as difficulty finding a new place to call home and the impact on future homeownership.

Throughout this book, we explored the different types of property liens, how they can impact property owners, and the options available for dealing with them. From tax lien nightmares to programs for delinquent property, we covered a wide range of topics to provide a comprehensive guide for navigating property tax liens.

Ultimately, the key takeaway is the importance of staying on top of tax payments and seeking professional help when needed to avoid the severe consequences of tax liens and foreclosures. By staying informed and taking proactive steps, property owners can protect their assets and secure their financial future.

About The Author

Maurice C. Hill is a man of many talents and experiences, including that of a former Adjunct Professor at Mercer University College of Professional Advancement and a decorated sailor who served in the United States Navy during the first Gulf War. Maurice's dedication to his country and service in the Navy instilled in him the values of discipline, teamwork, and commitment, which he continues to uphold in his personal and professional life.

After completing his military service, Maurice began his academic journey by earning undergraduate degrees in Business Administration and Education from Georgia State University. He later earned a Bachelor's degree in Business Management and a Master's degree in Business Administration from the University of Phoenix. Maurice's passion for counseling individuals and families led him to pursue a Master's degree in Clinical Mental Health Counseling from Mercer University, where he also studied Counselor Education and Supervision while in a Ph.D. program.

Maurice's vast knowledge and experience in various fields have made him a sought-after authority in his respective areas. He is currently a licensed real estate broker and a licensed professional counselor (LPC) in the state of Georgia, a National Certified Counselor (NCC), a member of the Dekalb Board of Realtors, the Georgia Association of Realtors, and the National Association of

Realtors. Maurice began his real estate career in 1997 and later became the chief executive officer (CEO) and qualifying broker of All Properties Professionals Realty in East Point, Georgia. He also serves as the founder and CEO of One United Publishing, where he helps business owners achieve their goals and aspirations through self-help books.

Maurice's dedication to helping others extends beyond his professional life. While in graduate school with a focus on training master's level clinical mental health counselors, Maurice became concerned about helping budding entrepreneurs who desire to own and operate their businesses. Inspired by the strong desire and sense of urgency related to helping business owners, Maurice decided to apply for and eventually enroll in the Harvard University entrepreneurship program. With his combined education and experience as an educator, business owner, and counselor, Maurice decided to write a group of self-help books.

Maurice has lectured nationally and internationally on various topics related to mental health counseling, including Vicarious Trauma, the Psychological Aspects of Multiculturalism in Counseling, and Trauma-Focused Cognitive Behavioral Therapy. He has been honored with numerous awards throughout his career, including The Empire Board of Realtist Million Dollar Club Award from 2000-2006 and the Dekalb Board of Realtors Pinnacle Award in 2020, 2021, and 2022. He is also a member of the Chi Sigma Iota

Maurice C. Hill

International Honor Society.

In addition to his professional accomplishments, Maurice is an avid traveler who has visited nearly 30 countries. His experiences abroad have enriched his understanding of humanity and the natural world. Studying the diverse cultures, histories, and socio-political landscapes of the places he has visited have deepened his love for humanity and nature. These experiences have opened his eyes to the complexity and beauty of our world and have inspired him to be a lifelong learner and advocate for positive change.

Maurice C. Hill is a remarkable individual who has impacted the lives of many through his passion, dedication, and expertise. His unwavering commitment to helping people achieve their goals and aspirations inspires others. With extensive knowledge and experience in multiple fields, Maurice is highly regarded as an authority and sought-after speaker. Additionally, Maurice has pursued his passion for flying airplanes by training at the Aviation Career Enrichment Inc in Atlanta, Georgia. His love for adventure and exploration, coupled with his dedication to his work, make him an inspiration to all. When he's not up in the air, Maurice enjoys spending quality time with his family.